88 KEYS TO LIVING A LONG AND PURPOSEFUL LIFE

HAZEL RAMSBOTHAM

The Produce My Book Promise:

Our goal at ProduceMyBook.com is to provide you with a proven sequence of steps and sub-steps to learn and apply new skills...faster.

Authors benefit from our process by having a completed book to call their own, in as little as 8 weeks, without ever typing a word of the manuscript.

We have made every effort to produce the content of this book using the exact words provided by the author during a series of intensive talkwriting sessions allowing all content to be produced within a few days. The result is a premium quality product in a concise but detailed format that could have a positive impact on your life if you put its suggestions into action.

c/o Produce My Book
PO Box 441024
Aurora, CO 80044
www.ProduceMyBook.com
crew@ProduceMyBook.com

CONTENTS

ACKNOWLEDGMENTS

First, I want to thank my mother, Daisy Mae Roby, for teaching me that I could do anything if I wanted to do it badly enough! Also deserving of recognition are my three brothers, Harold, James and Charles, to whom I looked up to all of my life. All three became colonels in the Air Force and the older two became outstanding citizens in their civilian lives after military service. Charles met his untimely death in Vietnam in 1967.

My five children, Roma, Randy, Ronda, Roy and Ree, have urged me for years to write my memoirs and they have been so supportive of anything I did. My whole life has been wrapped up in them.

Although Buddy Ramsbotham passed from this life in 2001, he gave me the most wonderful ten years of marriage, and showed me what marriage was really supposed to be.

Without the thousands of students I have taught over 74 years, many of whom have accomplished beautiful lives with their music, I wouldn't be here: Debra Walser-Augustus, Susan Hamilton-LeClair, Susan Hallam-Masson, the families of the Converses, Kasunicks, Zablockis and many more. (Others are named in the context of the book.)

Vergie Brannan of Lander, Wyoming, was always my "information bureau" when I needed anything pertaining to being a practical homemaker. Others in Lander, Wyoming were Doris Murray, a fabulous teacher who taught all my children either in school and/or Bible school and has been a friend for 60 years, and Mel and Dot Ashby. Mel helped in many ways and was a father to my children after their own father left the family and Dot is a precious friend and co-worker.

Rogers and June Bryant and Val and Nancy Milegar reached out to me when I first moved to Aurora, Colorado and have been loyal, supportive friends through the years. Recently, my walking partner, Gail Heiken, has added another dimension to my life!

My music colleagues: Doris Merritt, who taught me jazz piano and Nelita True, an accomplished Internationally known concert pianist, gave me encouragement and enjoyment of various kinds of music. Cindy Allor, of Aurora, Colorado, has been beyond supportive in our work together.

I want to thank Beth Gillard for being my real estate broker and manager of my properties which has freed me up to pursue other interests, and for William, (Bill) Seastrom for being my right hand man to help keep the household running smoothly. Thank you Daniel Julaton, my personal trainer, for showing me that I can develop muscles at 88 years old!

This book would not have been written had it not been for Marty Dickinson (ProduceMyBook.com), his wife Sue, and their talkwriting method. They are the most worthy of acknowledgement because they have guided me through the whole process. Barbara Peck, my professional photographer, not only did the cover photo, but she has been my fabulous mentor in Toastmasters from the beginning of that endeavor.

My sincerest thanks also goes to the dear friends and colleagues who wrote forewords for this book: Dr. Paul Williams, Loren Slocum-Lahav, Phyllis Pfeiffer, and Dr. Jason Geary.

I could go on and on listing the myriads of special people who have helped shape my life but these are a beginning. My Juice Plus team is extremely important to me!

Thank you all for blessing my life and being my friends!

FOREWORD
BY PAUL P. WILLIAMS, M.D.

I met Hazel several years ago because of our mutual association with The Juice Plus Company. We have spent time together in various settings, from small in-home events to conferences of thousands of people. In my role as a physician, I have tried to help people improve their chances of being as healthy as possible. Hazel does this as well in her work with Juice Plus, and she does it with a level of enthusiasm I have rarely seen in anyone else.

Hazel and I were once visiting in the home of a mutual friend when she fell, sustaining a serious injury to the side of her face. It took quite a bit of convincing, but eventually she agreed to be evaluated at the local hospital. She was admitted for xrays and observation (she didn't think this was necessary). In addition to the obvious significant bruising and swelling, she was found to have two broken bones in her face. During her overnight stay, she refused all offers of pain medication. She wanted to be alert to talk with everyone who came into her room – from housekeeping to doctors – about how much better off they would be if they had more nutrition from fruits and vegetables in their diets.

The "88 Keys" in this book are derived from experiences in Hazel's life. I think of them as educational experiences, and has she ever had an education! Every one of her 88 Keys offers something to be learned by everyone who reads her story.

Ultimately, Hazel is a teacher. After decades of teaching piano to an untold number of students, she now focuses her efforts on teaching anyone who will listen about the whole-food-based supplement Juice Plus and its proven health benefits. She spends every day doing her best to help others. I have benefitted greatly from being exposed to her vitality and her efforts to be a force for positive change in the lives of others. For this, I will always be grateful.

Dr. Paul Williams, Collierville, TN
1975 graduate of the West Virginia University School of Medicine, former Emergency Medicine practitioner, physician for several athletic teams and events, including the US International Roller Hockey Team, the 1996 Summer Olympics, numerous high school teams, and the Bell South Golf Classic. Dr. Williams is currently the Corporate Medical Director for NSA in Memphis, TN. His popular lectures have been attended by thousands around the U.S.

INTRODUCTION

Thousands of books are available about peoples' life stories and challenges, making money, living longer, and overcoming adversity to pursue one's life's purpose. How might this one be different? My 88 keys will provide the answer to that question.

My name is Hazel Roberts-Ramsbotham. I was born on April Fool's Day in 1930 and am 88 years *young* at the time of this writing. I never get sick. I do not take medication, and I grow most of my own food. Everything works, nothing hurts, and I still do 40 pushups, 40 sit-ups, and 40 squats daily—as I have for the past 36 years. When I speak on stage, sometimes to thousands of people, the audience always enjoys cheering-on the "old lady" to knock out more pushups than most of them only wish they could do at their age.

If you feel your energy decreasing with age year after year, take it from me. You need to start doing something differently now! It's never too late until it really is too late. The music only stops when you stop playing the music. It will be my honor to share my keys with you for lifelong health and longevity.

A cotton field in Texas was my first place of employment beginning at 6-years-old. From sunup to sundown, Monday through Saturday, my three older brothers and I would pick cotton alongside adults in 110-degree heat for $0.50 per 100 pounds. The last day I picked at age 11, I picked 250 pounds, and earned $1.25. After that, I started earning my own money by teaching piano. My love for music was my gateway to college and provided me with a means of income and fulfillment for the next 74 years as a nationally certified piano teacher. Today, I am retired from teaching to expand a business full-time that I started a few years ago as a health and wellness coach, author and speaker.

If you feel the pressures of money, debt, financial loss, and wonder if you will ever be free from living paycheck to paycheck (or worse), my keys to financial wealth will give you a whole new perspective and plan to consider.

People describe me with words like "adventurous," "a ball of fire," and "health nut." They are amazed at the things I have done since I turned 80, the time most people are slowing down. When I tell people that I visited Egypt in 2011 and rode a camel at age 81, they cannot believe it. I can tell you, riding a camel for more than a mile is not pleasant! They move both left legs and both right legs at the same time, unlike a horse, that staggers their front and back right and left legs. On a camel, you are rocking from right to left the entire time, and it's a rough ride. I do not recommend riding a camel to anyone for lengthy transportation! Like many things we would not want to do every day, like riding a camel, I am grateful for the adventures I continue to take and my desire to always expand, learn and grow every day.

I might be bold and brave today, but my beginnings were far from having high aspirations. An over-controlling mother, a 27 ½ year marriage that grew abusive, and absurdly primitive living conditions without running water or a furnace in a cold and remote area of Wyoming added to the challenge of raising five children. I had every reason to give up and just run away from it all. What I did instead will captivate and inspire you! If you feel you simply cannot go on, I will provide you with the keys to endure and continue when you need to and stand-up for yourself when it's time to.

Looking back, I see my life as a wonderful adventure, glittered with success patches along the way. I have re-written my life several times over the years, and I'm told my perseverance is inspirational and contagious. I have five amazing children whom I love and who love me back. I have found a purpose that gets me up every day and makes me want to grow professionally and personally by helping people around the world become healthy, wealthy, and wise. I have been very blessed.

My children have urged me to tell my story. They think people can learn and grow through hearing it. We live in such a different world now than when I was born. However, our dreams and our hurdles to get there are the same.

But stories are stories. How can my experiences help you in your life?

I hope that you will discover through these pages that you can do much more in this life than you think you can. If you are going through tough times today, there really is a brighter possibility for you tomorrow.

Life is like a musical composition that changes rhythm and direction at times but has the same themes woven together throughout the years and seasons. Tying this book to music and the 88 keys of a piano, the one thing that's remained consistent during my entire life, just makes sense.

In fact, MUSIC is not just a word, but an acronym for how all the keys in this book work together. I have used the five letters, M.U.S.I.C., to organize the 88 keys into a systematic method for you to achieve an abundant life with fulfilled purpose. You will be introduced to my stories, family, and friends I've met along the way and 88 specific keys to overcome any adversity, disappointment or challenge you may face throughout your youth or aging years with my M.U.S.I.C. system.

A piano has 88 keys that work in harmony together when played with timing, precision, and passion. Today, your lessons begin! Have a seat. Pull your stool up to the piano of life. Place your hands on the keys and your feet on the pedals. Get ready to play!

M.U.S.I.C.
PART 1: M
MIRACLE – MAGIC – MASTERMIND

You are a **Miracle**. Believe it. **Magic** in life only happens when you accept that there is a **Mastermind** that created you for a purpose.

CHAPTER 1: THE MAGIC OF WORK – THOSE COTTON-PICKING DAYS

One of my earliest memories is how Mother (as she was formally known in my house) always said to my three older brothers and me, "You can do anything you want in life, as long as you want it badly enough." During our growing up years, I did not understand how she could feel that way because we had so little. My father died on January 25 of 1936, and I had not yet reached my 6th birthday. Like most families in those days, we all relied on him to support us before he died. Although he rarely said it, we knew we all meant the world to him. Someone told me when I was much older, that I was the apple of his eye. But, at the time of his death, I was feeling abandoned, alone and terrified. Who else would take care of me?

When he died, everything changed. I remember the moment I realized nobody was going to make a living for us; that we had to do it ourselves. Mother, my three older brothers, Harold, James, Charles, and me, Hazel; that's all there was. A woman and four children under the age of 12, in 1936 - that's a burden for everyone involved, even the five-year-old.

Key #1: You really can do anything you want in life, as long as you want it badly enough, (plus my addition to the saying) even when surprises try to convince you otherwise.

Our mother would never have taken a handout. We never

went to soup lines for our meals. A lot of people did at that time, but somehow we managed to survive without having to do it.

I remember thinking, "Oh, what are we going to do?" Even at age 5, I knew we had to do something to survive. So, when Mother told my brothers and me to go to the cotton fields near Commerce, Texas where we lived and pick cotton over the summer, I took it as an opportunity for the family. I didn't see it as a punishment. It was an opportunity to make our way together.

Key #2: Some things need to be done without complaint.

Picking cotton was never something I loved to do, but it was just something that we did for the family at the time. Mother seemed to know the exact motivation that my brothers and I needed. She only needed to tell me to do my best and to make sure to pick as much or more than my brothers could! I decided they were not going to do anything better than I could do.

My brothers were tougher nuts to crack. I remember that Mother would stand at the door as we left for the cotton fields and tell the boys, "You pick more cotton than Hazel does, or you'll get the whip when you come home." That was the motivation they needed to stay focused on the job and not go crazy running up and down the cotton rows.

Key #3: Avoiding pain motivates everyone to act.

That was the way it was for six years, from 1936-1941. I was six when I started, and I picked cotton until I was 11.

Cotton picking was long, hard work in the hot Texas summer. We got up very early in the morning; before daylight. Mother always made us a big breakfast of biscuits, bacon, and eggs, and then we dressed in our cotton-picking clothes.

I remember we had to be covered from head to toe to avoid sunstroke. I wore pants to protect my legs from the bugs and a bonnet to shade my face. In those days, girls wore short little cute dresses all the time, so that was humbling for me. I did not like boy's pants at all! But they were necessary. And we wore closed-toe shoes and long-sleeved shirts. All that clothing sure got hot in the 110-degree temperatures we worked in, even though it was all light-weight cloth. I remember sweating all the time. The sweat just soaked our bodies throughout the day as we picked the cotton. What a pleasant respite it was when any breeze came along because it would cool us off.

There were a lot of other people in the fields, picking the cotton, children and grownups alike. It became kind of a community thing over the summer. We could visit during our thirty-minute lunch break in the shade of the cotton wagons. Mother packed sandwiches wrapped in wax paper for lunch for us. They were usually peanut butter or peanut butter and jelly, but sometimes Mother would make peanut butter and mashed banana sandwiches. We *loved* those sandwiches.

After the 30-minute lunch break, it was back to picking. The only time we got a drink of water was when we filled our sack with cotton. A cotton sack measured a little longer than five feet long and was made from canvas so that it would not tear when dragged across the ground. There was a hole in the fabric at the top of the bag, creating a sling we could put around our neck. In that way, we would drag the bag along the ground as we slowly moved down the cotton row from plant to plant.

The cotton grows in a protective pod, called a boll. As the cotton ripens, the fluffy white fibers expand until they look like cotton candy and split the boll apart until it looks like a four-leaf clover. The boll is surrounded by sharp stickers that could puncture the skin. So, we had to be very careful to grab the plant in such a way that we could pull the cotton out of the boll without touching the stickers.

You have to bend over all the time to pick cotton. When we got tired of bending over, we would get down on our knees and crawl for a while. Some of the people picking cotton with my brothers and me had knee pads so they could crawl more comfortably, but we didn't have any. So, I would crawl for a while, but had to get up on my feet after a short time because my knees hurt so much.

We made our way down the cotton rows, with the five-foot-long bag slung around our necks so that our arms were free to pick. The bag had to be so full we couldn't get it any fuller. We would drag it to the wagon in the middle of the pasture because it was too heavy to carry. The overseer would weigh it, and then we got a drink from the water barrel with a dipper that everybody else used. We never gave germs a thought. We were healthy. We didn't have to worry about getting sick. That was the only time we were able to take a drink throughout the day.

We would be paid every day because there would be a different group of pickers every day, so you never knew who would show up the next day. Sometimes there would be ten pickers, sometimes 30. You might be picturing a field full of blacks or Mexicans, but no. I never even met a black person until many years later when I moved to Wyoming, and there was one black family in town. I never met a Mexican until much later. We were just a group of non-privileged white folks working as a community in the harsh hot Texas sun.

It was a long day. We were there until sundown. When the sun started going down, we would return to the wagon, have the rest of our cotton weighed, and receive our pay for that day. We put the coins in our pockets, went home, and gave it to

Mother. We would never take any money out for ourselves. It was for the family. I think we knew that we were in survival mode together, and it took all of us to make it work.

Key #4: Your family is in it together.

During those six years, Mother was getting her teaching certificate and working where she could as well. As far as I recall, our family was never in want. We were just like all the other families at that time. We had what we needed, and that was enough. I don't recall ever needing or wanting anything in particular, except for a stuffed animal. I do remember thinking it would be nice to have a stuffed animal.

Key #5: Be satisfied with what you have.

By the time I was 11 years-old, mother had her teaching certificate and was teaching school. My brothers had gone to West Texas to work the wheat harvest. So, I was home alone that summer and Mother informed me that I would not have to pick cotton anymore if I didn't want to. Well, that was a no-brainer because I certainly didn't want to!

Looking back, I see God's hand at work during those early years molding me into the person I am today. Mother's repeated message that I can do anything I want if I want it badly enough has become my driving force. And I learned a lot of valuable lessons very early on that have gotten me through tough times over the years; lessons such as self-respect and satisfaction in a job well done.

My faith in God has grown since those early years because I learned that God would take care of us. I believe that. I think that if you live right, like the Bible teaches you should live, God will bless you. He can make miracles happen. Changes and results might take longer than you might expect, but they can happen for you eventually. I'm thinking of the story of

Joseph in the Bible. He went through many adversities before finally overcoming mistreatment, rejection, and abuse. But God was with him, and eventually, he rose above it all.

Key #6: We know that God causes everything to work together for the good of those who love God and are called according to his purpose for them. (Romans 8:28 NLT)

CHAPTER 2: THE MASTERMIND'S CALL TO MUSIC

You are a Miracle. God made you for a purpose, and you need to find out what that purpose is. What many people do not realize is that your purpose can change throughout your life, depending on your age and situation at the time. I do not believe we see miracles as they did in the New Testament, but God *does* direct our lives if we listen to his instructions, obey them, and do what he says.

My youngest daughter Ree found her purpose by the time she was three years old. My kids went to Bible Camp every year, and the year she was three there was a missionary from Malaysia visiting. In his message, he had described how part of their mission was to buy Bibles for the children in Malaysia. After his message, Ree, Roy, and Ronda sang, and the missionary gave each one ten cents for their contribution.

Ree gave her dime right back to the missionary so that he could use it to buy Bibles for the children in Malaysia. Even at that early age, she was very mission minded. Now she has been in Brazil with her husband Allen nearly 32 years as missionaries. She listened to God's call for her and knew very early what she was meant to do.

Key #7: God will take care of us if we trust and behave according to His will.

I have found my purpose. In fact, I found it more than once. As a child, my goal was to live a good honest life and help our family to survive the depression. As a wife to my first husband, and mother, my purpose was to raise my five children and teach them the right way to live. And now I feel my purpose is to encourage people all around the world to be healthy, wealthy and wise.

God has blessed me with the gift of music that has been a universal thread throughout my life; something that has formed how I have carried out my purpose for over eighty years.

I knew as early as age six that I wanted to be a music teacher. I don't know where that came from because I wasn't acquainted with any music teachers at the time. In 1936, I had barely any exposure to music. That was even before the Grand Ole Opry.

I remember us gathering around the radio to listen to my Uncle Eddie Dean on the WLS Barn Dance from Chicago on Saturday night. The Barn Dance and singing at church were about the only exposures to music I had. But, I guess God must have implanted music in my DNA. Music was always important to me, and I took to it easily.

Key #8: Pay attention to the things for which you are passionate about.

When I was in first grade, my teacher taught us a new song every day. I would come home and pick out the tune on Mother's piano. And then I got bored with just the melody, so I started making up something to play along with the left hand. I was playing by ear at six years old, and that has always been part of my music. Mother was very concerned, because, in her day, someone who played music by ear had a difficult time learning to read music. So, she worried that I would never learn to read music. Her worry was unfounded because, of course, I did learn to read music and eventually studied music in college. But I did not have that kind of training growing up.

When I was nine, there was a high school girl who could play quite well, so Mother had me take lessons from her. I took lessons throughout the winters that I was 9 and 10, but she traveled in the summer. Then, her family moved far enough away so that I could no longer study with her.

After she moved, some girls asked me if I would teach them piano. Now that my teacher had left, I became the one that accompanied the choirs at school. Even though I hadn't had a lot of lessons, I was the only one left that played the piano. So, they came and asked me to teach them. I had no idea how to do that. I could hardly read music myself. But I told them it would be $.25 a lesson, and I showed them what I knew. Some of them went on and majored in music in college, so I must have done something right.

I found out quickly that I could make as much money from five lessons in the comfort of my home as I did all day in the hot cotton fields. Not to mention, I could keep all my own money. This launched my music teaching career!

Key #9: Trust yourself to do the best job you can.

When I was 12, a friend of mine had a little tiny 12 bass accordion. I thought it was fascinating. I loved it. I wanted to learn to play the accordion a lot.

That summer, Mother and I went to Dallas to be near my Aunt Lorene. My two younger brothers were in West Texas at my uncle's place, and my oldest brother had entered the military, so it was just Mother and me. We found an apartment, and Mother and I babysat the owner's five-year-old daughter to pay our rent.

As we drove into Dallas that summer, I remember seeing a great big sign that said Whittle Music Company. I turned to Mother and said, "I want to learn to play the accordion." Once we got settled, she took me to the Whittle Music Company to check it out. We rented a 12-bass accordion with 25 treble keys, and the instructor gave me a book to practice with at home between lessons.

The next week, my teacher asked to speak to Mother. She stopped by after work, and he told her that I had already outgrown the 12-bass accordion. He said I had played everything I could play on it and needed to get the next size up, which was a 48 bass.

Mother got me the larger accordion, and I had five lessons before the summer was over and we returned home. I soon outgrew even that 48 bass accordion, and as soon as I could afford it, I bought myself a full-size 120 bass accordion with a full set of major and minor chords. I played that accordion crazily. I played so much that I was soon able to play just about anything by ear. If I knew it, or you could sing it, I could play it!

I remember my brother Harold was coming home from the military, and he loved the song *Under the Double Eagle*, so I learned it so that I could play it for him. He was so proud of me.

When I graduated from high school, it never occurred to me to do anything but major in music. But, by that time, I did not even have a piano to practice on. Mother had sold it when I was a sophomore in high school because she didn't want to move it when we moved from Cunningham to Iowa Park Texas in 1944, which was several hundred miles away.

I hadn't had any professional lessons to speak of, although I had been teaching neighborhood children and school friends all along.

Most people that became music majors in college started formal training at six years old and learned a full repertoire. I knew nothing about repertoire. I barely even knew who Bach was until I attended college.

Looking back now is intriguing to remember how inadequate I felt over the years teaching piano. Teaching the piano was precisely what God was leading me to do.

Key #10: Follow where God leads you.

I'm grateful I saw my eldest daughter Roma's talent and nurtured it early because she did not need to question her ability as I did. Roma was somewhat of a child prodigy. She was playing concert caliber material by the time she was 11 years old. She just wowed everybody when she performed.

In 1968, when she was a sophomore in High School, someone heard Roma play and suggested she enter the Casper Symphony Contest. She performed Beethoven's First Piano Concerto in the contest, but with a snowstorm moving in, we decided to leave before the awards were announced. We were on our way to drop Roma off at Interlochen Arts Academy in Traverse City Michigan where she transferred for her final two years of High School.

We flew from Casper to Traverse City Michigan, and when we arrived at the Interlochen Academy, there was a telegram waiting that said Roma had won the Casper Symphony Contest. She earned $500 scholarship and the chance to play with the Casper Symphony.

Roma said, "They can keep the money; I just want to play with the symphony!" Ah, youth. I was glad to get the money because it went toward her college! But we were all excited the next April when she performed with the Symphony.

While Roma was attending Interlochen, I learned of the Spencer-Penrose Contest which was a multi-state contest with local, state, and regional levels named after two prominent families in Colorado at the time. I talked to the head of the music department at the University of Wyoming about whether Roma should participate, and he advised against it as it was highly competitive.

But, he had never heard Roma play. I decided to go ahead and have her come home and compete. She won an all-expense paid trip to Central City and performed in the contest in Denver Colorado. She won $500 again for a first-place finish.

Key #11: Seek advice but be willing to decide against that advice.

Roma loved competition. She was always nervous and never felt she should win. Every time she won she would say, "They must have made a mistake, it couldn't be me!" But competing was a tremendous help for her to realize her God-given ability. All my children have competed in various contests throughout their lives, and they all have developed incredible self-esteem; something I lacked for much of my life. Over and over, I see God's hand at work in my life, as I believe He gave me the ability to recognize my children's strengths early and help them find their purpose in life.

CHAPTER 3: THE MIRACLE OF BELIEVING IN YOURSELF

I remember a piano student once asked me if I thought she should major in music. I told her no. If she were supposed to major in music, she wouldn't have to ask. You have to do it because that's the only way you want to live. That's the only way you can do it. As I said in the last chapter, by the time I was a sophomore in High School, I knew I wanted to be a music major in college. It was the same for Roma. But none of my other children got a degree in music, although they all studied piano and other instruments throughout their youth.

You have to listen to your passions to discover your purpose. There is no competition here. Everybody has different talents, and you should never compare yourself to others. Ever. You need to focus on being the best *you* that you can be. Everybody has their own abilities, and you need to develop what you can do, not what somebody else can do.

Key #12: Don't compare yourself to anyone else. Focus on being the best you can be.

If there is one thing I have discovered as a piano teacher over all these years, it's the importance for parents to encourage their children to believe in themselves even when no one else thinks they have a chance at success. As a teacher or a coach, you never know what a kid can do. I have found that the most talented kids can be some of the laziest, and the one who struggles may be the kid who ultimately excels.

I remember the Pfeiffenberger family taught me a great deal about perseverance and never giving up. David was an emotionally upset young man after the death of his father. His mother insisted that David continue with his piano lessons, but he wouldn't practice and barely learned anything we went through in class. He couldn't even identify if a note was on a space or a line in a score. It was terrible.

His mother begged me to keep working with him. I did, but he wasn't progressing at the same level as his peers in group lessons. I tried to arrange my students in groups according to their age and ability, but as the years went on, fellow students would move on to a different group and David would have to stay behind. Eventually, he would get too big, and I had to advance him to the next group, even though he didn't fit in.

This continued for several years, and David's mother insisted that he stick with it despite his poor performance. But then, something happened. As part of the group training, I had my students write a composition every year. They had to write it by hand - no computer programs or other shortcuts. I made them write it out in longhand and be able to play it.

The first year his group worked on compositions, David wrote a simple piece that was eight measures long. It had a catchy tune with a little syncopation to it. David was so proud of that composition. All of a sudden, he just flourished. David advanced up to the high school group quickly and became one of my most accomplished composers. He composed pieces that were eight pages long, and he wowed everybody with his work by the time he finished high school.

David is my most striking example of someone who seemed to have no chance at success that, with encouragement, turned it around. Looking back, I think his father's death hurt him so much that he was unable to grow mentally for a long time. But his mother never told him he couldn't do it, and neither did I. We believed in David until he believed in himself.

Key #13: Allow others to believe in you until you can believe in yourself.

It all goes back to doing your best, at whatever you decide to do. Never do anything half-heartedly. If you want to be a museum director, you need to study history. If you like computer programming, devour everything you can find about computer programming. Once you discover your passion, it won't be hard to do. You don't have to beat yourself up with a stick to succeed at what you love. You will just do it and put your best foot forward.

Believing in yourself was my doctrine for the entire 74 years I taught music, and it hasn't changed since I retired to pursue my current career with Juice Plus. I have discovered that you need to believe in four things to be successful in the Juice Plus business: the product, the process, the company, and yourself.

That last one is always the hardest. You have to believe in yourself. All the other stuff is science. There is proven evidence on which you can rely.

Believing in yourself can be confusing and unclear, especially when you have not had encouragement and training throughout your life. Most people do not have any belief in themselves. David didn't, but I, his mom, and his peers in the group lesson believed for him.

My weekly group lessons were an essential part of my curriculum. Children tend to learn some things easier and more quickly from their peers than from a teacher or parent. The groups were small enough that the kids got to know each other well. Many of my students have become friends for life, and they still keep in touch with their group lesson peers after all these years. Their genuine encouragement helped them all build the self-esteem they needed to believe in themselves.

David was no exception, even though it took a bit longer to get through his shell. His friends encouraged him. He saw what they were doing, and at some point, he said I can do this too. And he did!

Key #14: Let the positive energy of a group propel you forward when you can't do it on your own.

I've seen it happen over and over. I think the Mastermind uses other people to provide the gentle nudge of motivation that we need to find and fulfill the purpose he has for us. Often, we mistake that supernatural nudge for human interference unless we stay open to it.

When I first learned about Juice Plus, I sure did not recognize God's encouraging hand. I was a hard nut to crack, I'll tell you! But, you would never know it to look at me now. And I'm not the only one. Many people never intended to get involved in Juice Plus, but, thanks to the persistence of others, finally saw what it can do and how it can help people.

That thought is the concluding message I want to convey in this initial step – M – to a Musical Life. The Mastermind put us here on earth to help people. That is our ultimate purpose.

Many people believe the goal is to be happy, but I argue otherwise. To serve God and man is the desire He has put in our heart, and we will only honestly be satisfied if we do it. That is what people misunderstand. They think God is restrictive and keeps them from having fun and doing what they want to do. They want to do whatever feels right and have God approve. It's like letting a toddler do whatever he wants even though his parent knows it is dangerous.

No! That's letting the prisoners run the asylum! God tells us what we should do, and if we do it, we will be happy. It's not the other way around. That's why he gives us rules and regulations because he knows that that's what will make us happy.

King Solomon is known as one of the wealthiest and wisest men who lived. And yet, he spent much of his life searching for the key to happiness. He tried everything – food, women, drink, wild living and more, but was never satisfied. His story is in the Book of Ecclesiastes. That book tells us that after all his searching, King Solomon finally summed it up: "That's the whole story. Here now is my final conclusion: Fear God and obey his commands, for this is everyone's duty" (Ecclesiastes 12:13 NLT).

That's it. If we follow Solomon's advice, we will be happy, and we will make the world happy. Stop searching for happiness. Happiness is like a butterfly. If you are chasing the butterfly all the time, it is just going to fly away. But if you sit quietly, the butterfly will come and land on your shoulder.

Key #15: Fear God and obey his commands, for this is everyone's duty.

Roma performing at the first benefit concert to raise money to buy a piano for the Aurora Public Library, a fundraiser that Hazel spearheaded

Back: Jonathon & Ronda, Jan & Randy, Allen & Ree
Front Row: Roy, Shane, Hazel, Roma

M.U.S.I.C.
PART 2: U
UNDERWRITER – UNAFRAID – UNSHAKEN

While God created you for a purpose, he made you the **Underwriter** of your life. You have to be **Unafraid** and **Unshaken** in your willingness to do whatever it takes to fulfill the purpose God gave you.

HAZEL RAMSBOTHAM

FOREWORD
BY LOREN SLOCUM-LAHAV

There are some people who you fall in love with right away, for their infectious energy and inspiring nature. Hazel Roberts-Ramsbotham is one of those people.

I first met Hazel in Dubai, where we were both attending a Juice Plus conference. It was hard not to notice the beautiful, 87-year-old woman working out in the hotel gym as if she was 37. I knew instantly that she was someone who I wanted to meet.

During our first conversation, Hazel talked about her kids, her history of teaching piano for 74 years and her upcoming "piano birthday." And she let me in on her little secret for staying in such great shape: Since her 52nd birthday, she had done 40 pushups, 40 sit-ups and 40 squats—every single day. Her son, a physical training coach at the time, had told her that if she stuck to that exercise routine, that she'd be able to travel and live the life she really wanted into her 80s and beyond. And so she did it—with astounding results. This story is just one testament to Hazel's strong commitment to her vision.

For the rest of our time in Dubai, I invited Hazel to spend time with my friends and me. Not only did we enjoy Hazel's company, but she was up for everything. From riding camels to sand dune bashing (a thrill ride through the desert in an SUV, much like a roller coaster ride), Hazel loved every minute. It became clear to us just how much she embraces every moment and lives her life to the absolute fullest. Her energy and attitude alone will inspire you to live your very best life.

Since that week, Hazel and I have stayed friends. I invited her to speak on a panel at my Juice Plus Bootcamp, where she inspired the attendees to take their lives and businesses to the next level. I started doing what I call "Healthy Hazels"—40 pushups, 40 sit-ups and 40 squats—and I've shared this exercise routine with people all around the world. I share Hazel's story not only to help people stay physically fit, but to show them what is possible in life when you follow through on your vision. As you will discover in Find Your Music, Hazel does not do anything half-heartedly. Once she decides what she wants, she goes after it at full speed until she gets it—and after reading this book, you'll want to do the same.

In my 28 years of working in personal development, I've met many authors, speakers and coaches, and I can tell you that Hazel is a true visionary. She has lived a life unlike many of us have experienced, from picking cotton at the age of six to help support her family to becoming an award-winning piano teacher and starting a new career in her 80s. There were many challenges that stood in her way, such as her unsupportive mother, her abusive marriage and financial hardship. Through these challenges, Hazel learned valuable lessons that shaped her into the strong, accomplished person she is today. In the pages that follow, Hazel will pass those lessons along to you. I encourage you to apply these teachings instantly, so you can transform your own life into one brimming with purpose and fulfillment.

Throughout her book, Hazel proves that we don't have to slow down as we age—in fact, our lives can become richer with every passing year. Hazel looks great, feels great, travels the world and is constantly having new adventures. She'll explain how you too can live a long, healthy and vibrant life, full of meaning and joy. It doesn't matter where you are in your life right now, this book will help you get exactly where you want to go.

Not only is Hazel an amazing leader and teacher, but she's an incredible mother, grandmother and friend. It's been an honor getting to know Hazel, and I know you will love getting to know her too.

Here's to discovering your purpose, following your passion and living a life that you love—at every age.

Loren Slocum-Lahav is an international personal development speaker, author, dedicated mom of 3 and wife.

HAZEL RAMSBOTHAM

CHAPTER 4: BECOMING THE UNDERWRITER OF YOUR LIFE

While it's true that we have a Mastermind leading us to fulfill our purpose, we must collaborate with Him to fulfill that purpose. The burning passion you have is a sign to get to work and make it happen. Be your own underwriter. Create your destiny. No one wants it as much as you do.

Key #16: Be your own underwriter. No one wants it as much as you do.

The ability to actualize your future will evolve gradually. I am giving this advice looking back at my life over the past eighty years. Achieving the dreams I had as a girl did not happen smoothly. In fact, I discovered two things early in my life: first, the world is flawed, and second, we are not always in control of our circumstances.

Discovering the fire in my belly for music did not take long. By the time I was a teenager, I knew I wanted to study music beyond high school. I dabbled in teaching piano to my friends and neighbors and even taught accordion at a music store called Norsworthy Music Center in Wichita Falls, Texas during my high school years. But, more than anything, I wanted to attend college to engross myself in music.

I enrolled in Harden College, a two-year community college

that eventually became Midwestern University in Wichita Falls, Texas, on a full scholarship. I had a job as a student assistant for the head of the music department. I would tutor the freshmen students in music theory. I had no formal music training, and yet I was teaching them musical theory!

During those first two years of college in Wichita Falls, it seemed as though my life was on-track to achieve the goals I had set so early in life. It did not come easy, even though I had a scholarship. I attended all my classes, worked for 2-3 hours each day on schoolwork and piano practice. Then I worked as a student assistant and continued teaching at the Norsworthy Music Center to earn more money. I wanted to transfer to North Texas Teacher's College in Denton, Texas after my two years in Wichita Falls because their music department had a reputation as an up-and-comer in musical education. So, I was saving for that. And, I was still living at home with Mother, so at the end of every long day, I would climb on the Continental Trailways bus to head for home.

Key #17: Don't be afraid to work hard for what you want.

As mentioned earlier, I "wanted" to transfer to Denton, Texas to attend North Texas Teacher's College. But, there was a big wall in my path. Mother, the same person who raised me thinking I could do anything I wanted if I worked hard enough, wouldn't let me go to Denton! She didn't want me to leave home. Suddenly, I found myself not in control of what I wanted to do.

I never had a bedroom of my own. I always shared my room with my mother. While living in the small quarters when working the cotton fields, my three brothers slept in one bed. My mother and I slept in another. She and I shared a bed from the time I was six years old. Part of Mother probably didn't want me to leave because it would have changed her life so dramatically. And, Mother worked from the old-school philosophy that the girl in the family was supposed to stay home and take care of her parents. That mindset came from the era she grew up in, and I know that is what she thought I should do.

Mother's demeanor towards me changed from supportive to calculating in my teens when I became interested in boys. She was all for me dating anybody as long as I did not genuinely care about them. But, if she thought I was beginning to show affection for a particular boy, she would look for all kinds of things wrong with him. I suppose she was afraid that I would not be around anymore if I married.

Regardless of her motivation, Mother took every opportunity she could to thwart my goal to attend school at Denton. I finally talked her into travelling there with me so that we could check out the school in person. We consulted with the school administrators, and they said that I could attend the school, but they could not guarantee a scholarship until I had been there for at least one semester. They wanted to see how I managed the first semester and, if I did well, they would be willing to negotiate grants or scholarships with me.

I loved the music department there, and I thought it would be heaven to go to Denton and live in a dorm. I had enough money to pay for my first semester because I had worked so hard and saved. Mother would not have had to spend anything. Truth be told, she never spent a penny on me. I had worked and made my own money since I was 11. I bought my own clothes and shoes. I paid for all my entertainment. She didn't need to buy anything for me and was used to it. So, I felt pretty independent.

The possibilities were so exciting, and I was ready to go immediately! But Mother didn't want me to go and began a campaign to convince me it would not work out. "What if you don't get a scholarship?" she would say. "You will just have to come home, and all your money will be gone. You would feel like a complete failure."

Her words were like sticking a dagger in my heart. She wore me down. I was convinced I could not handle the financial pressure or guilt brought on by Mother. So, I never did attend school in Denton.

Key #18: Don't allow the motivations of others to keep you from achieving your goals.

Right around this time, I was dating Quentin Roberts, who was working at the telephone company. He was courting me heavily to marry him and had plans to move to Missouri to attend college on the GI Bill. He sent me letters begging me to marry him and go away to school, but I never saw one of them. I didn't know it at the time, but Mother was confiscating the letters as they arrived at my house. Unfortunately, for her, that strategy backfired. I figured, moving out of the house to live with Quentin would be so much better than having to live at home. So, I got married. Not my brightest move, but that is another story.

Key #19: Never marry for anything but love.

My mother couldn't say anything good about Quentin. When I told her I was getting married, she had a fit and went into a temper tantrum. She was so critical. And she wasn't above using the guilt card, either!

I remember she was remodeling the house at that time. She cried for weeks, saying, "How can you leave? I'm remodeling for you!" The day before my marriage, she had me down on the floor painting the baseboards. A friend of mine came over to see me, and there I was, down on the floor. "What in the world are you doing," she cried, "...painting on the day before your wedding! Why don't you just elope?" Mother attacked, chased her out, and I kept on painting.

Key #20: Don't let guilt hold you back from your dreams.

Quentin and I married, but it was not until he left our family in 1977 that I started to get my footing and command my circumstances. Until then, my children and I did as Quentin directed, which took us in a hundred different directions.

If you are floundering and wondering if you can ever take charge and achieve your goals, let me assure you that it is okay to start gradually. Lao Tzu said, "A journey of a thousand miles begins with a single step." A baby step may be small, but it still moves you forward. The reason we have the challenges is to make us tough. If nothing ever went awry, we would be wimps. We have to have trials to make us strong and sturdy. You will not like the difficulty and stress at the time. But take it from someone who's been there, you will look back at it and say, "Yeah, I grew from that."

Key #21: Suffering produces endurance, and endurance produces character, and character produces hope (Romans 5: 3-4 NLT)

Mother and Me

CHAPTER 5: UNSHAKEN – MOTHER AND ME

My rapport with Mother was challenging over the years. I was the only girl out of four children, and she was a strict disciplinarian when we were young. I remember she would criticize me for everything. She didn't criticize the boys, but oh my goodness! I could do nothing right, and it was difficult.

You see, I was raised to always do what I was told to do. When someone in authority told me to do something, I didn't question it or complain. I just did what I was told.

For much of my life, I was entirely subservient to my mother, my brothers, and my first husband. Mother hated Quentin, and after he left the family, the first thing she said to me was, "I told you so." The problem my mother had with Quentin is that he wanted to control me as much as mother did. I felt like I was a referee between the two for my entire married life.

As hard to please as she was, I don't want to paint a disturbing picture of Mother because she was an honorable woman and took care of my brothers and me after my father died. Rather than put us in an orphan home as many widows did during the depression, Mother said, "NO WAY! If we go down, we go down together." She taught me about hard work, commitment, and dedication. In many ways, Mother was a beautiful person, and I loved her dearly.

Key #22: Look for the good in everyone, even if you have to look deep.

Mother taught me needlework at an early age, and I have enjoyed it my entire life. I learned embroidery and needlepoint at six years old and started crocheting when I was 12. I have crocheted miles and miles of thread. I have made four full-size bedspreads, six tablecloths, and more doilies than I can count. I crochet most of my gifts, especially for weddings and baby showers.

When I was 11, I stopped picking cotton over the summer, and I remember saying something to Mother that I had never said before and I've never said since. That was, "I don't have anything to do."

Mother suggested I make a quilt. I thought nobody made quilts but Grandmas. I never thought I could make a quilt. But she had some old sugar sacks she had saved (in those days sugar came in white cloth bags), and Mother thought they would be perfect for a quilt block.

Mother showed me how to cut out a Dutch doll quilt block, which is what is called an applique quilt. That means you sew the pieces of the block onto a solid square, which is what we used the sugar sacks for. A Dutch doll quilt block is a silhouette of a girl in a bonnet and dress. The bonnet, face, arms, and feet are all one solid color, and then a print fabric is used for the dress. Each block can be a different combination of colors and patterns. The result is a lovely finished quilt if you can harmonize the colors and patterns.

I made that first quilt top at age 11 and, surprisingly, the colors matched perfectly. I didn't realize at the time that that was unusual, but people who have seen it since then (yes, I still have it!) are amazed that I could match those colors as I did. There are twenty blocks, and every block is different. But they are all the Dutch girl quilt blocks, and they all coordinate together beautifully.

I am still very proud of that quilt today, and I'll always remember being 11 years old that summer and catching the quilting bug. Not only did I make the Dutch Girl quilt pieces, but I completed the pieces for a second quilt as well. That quilt was called 'Road to Oklahoma,' and instead of applique, it is what is called a pieced quilt, meaning that the pieces of fabric were sewn together to make a square, rather than starting with a solid square and adding on the appliques.

After the summer, I put the pieces of those quilts away and didn't think about them again, until the summer that I got my master's degree in 1967. Mother came to see me in Lander, and she noticed my bedding was getting frayed. I told her I needed to budget some extra money to replace it, and Mother reminded she had those quilt blocks I had made when I was 11. She suggested she set them together and have them quilted for me as a Christmas gift.

I forgot all about our discussion until Christmas time came along and a big box from Mother appeared on my doorstep. When I opened it up, I was amazed at how beautiful it was. I don't remember before then ever seeing a brand-new quilt never used. Neither had my oldest daughter Roma, who was 14 at the time. She immediately wanted to make a quilt. We had just newly decorated her room in turquoise and white, so Roma and I made a Dutch doll quilt together in turquoise and white.

After we had the pieces made, I realized I had no idea how to put them together into quilts. Quentin went to the lumberyard and bought wood to make a quilting frame and Roma and I learned to finish the quilts together.

It is special to be able to share something I learned with my mother the summer I was 11 with my daughter all those years later. Since that first summer, I have made 59 quilts total, either by myself or with my children or Mother. Quilting is addictive!

When Mother noticed my renewed interest in quilting, she sent me some quilt block patterns and pictures she had saved from the newspapers dating back to 1936, and I used those patterns. Quilting was not as popular in the 1960s and 1970s as it is today, and you couldn't find patterns and supplies as easily. Despite other challenges I may have had with Mother, she was always aware of and engaged in pursuing my interests, which I appreciate.

Even though I was the only girl in the family, Mother did not coddle me by any stretch of the imagination. My brothers shared with me long after Mother died that she often talked about and bragged on me to other people, but I never knew it at the time. Mother never reinforced compliments I received from other people and would shush them up immediately when giving me personal praise. She didn't want me to think I was special because of my looks, but rather to behave myself. Pretty is as pretty does.

I think she went overboard in that regard, but it is easy to go overboard the other way also. Everyone knows those parents who lead their children to believe they are so cute and perfect that they can do no wrong, and the kids don't learn anything that way about getting along in the real world. The first time something or someone slaps them down, they don't know how to handle it. So, while Mother exaggerated it the opposite way, I certainly developed a tough skin which has helped me survive over the years.

I remember feeling like I was in the shadow of my brothers. They all became Colonels in the Air Force, and Harold and James had successful careers after retiring from the military as well. They were always valedictorian of their class, and I never felt anywhere near as successful as my brothers were. Mother would compound my feelings of inferiority with her talk about them. After she died, I learned she had similar conversations with my brothers about me, but while she was alive we did not know that, and there was always a rift between us. Thankfully, my brothers and I have since become very close.

Having Mother come to Denver to live with me was one of the hardest things I ever did in my life. By Fall, 1984, when Mother was 86, she was unable to live on her own in West Texas. I had made the eleven-hour drive to Texas that year to check on her at least monthly, and sometimes even more often.

My brothers had found an assisted living place for her in Texas, but she was just at that in-between stage where she did not need nursing care, but she could not be on her own either. So, I urged her to come and live with me.

Mother moved to Denver on Thanksgiving Day, 1984, to see if she could handle the cold here. She had never lived outside of Texas, and she thought it would be too cold for her here in Denver. She agreed to stay a month, and if she didn't freeze to death, she would move. I remember telling her, "You know, we have furnaces up here. Our homes are heated!" She had never had more than a wood stove her entire life.

Having Mother move in with me was the right thing to do, but it was very challenging. I was in my fifties by this time, but she still treated me like a child. She thought that we would spend lots of time together doing things like baking cookies and having fun. So, she was a little disappointed that I couldn't be with her all the time when she saw how many hours I worked every day. She surprised me once by telling me with admiration that none of my sisters-in-law (my brother's wives) would be able to make it through even one of my days.

Key #23: You never know who you are making an impression on, so always act in a way that will leave a good impression.

It was a trial to have Mother living in my house. My children were not close to her at all. I remember one road trip where my second daughter, Ronda, and I took Mother to Texas to meet the family of Ronda's fiancé. On the way, the car started acting up, and Mother blamed Ronda for the car trouble. Ronda didn't have anything to do with it! Her tirade got to Ronda. She stormed into the motel room that night and exclaimed, "How in the world do you put up with that? How could you be brought up with that kind of behavior and be like you are? No wonder you married dad!"

My youngest son, Roy did not get along well with Mother either. He was still living at home and attending College at Metropolitan State University when Mother lived with us. Mother would tell me Roy should not be living at home; that he was too old to stay at home. I told her that Roy was in college and working to pay tuition. But he reminded her of my first husband, Quentin, and they never got along because of it. Roy asked me several times if I was sure she was my mom. He told me there isn't a bone in my body like Mother.

One day, Roy was in my studio working on a college paper using my typewriter and Mother was sitting in the kitchen as I cooked. She told me that if I had listened to her before I married Quentin, I wouldn't be in the mess I was in. I wouldn't have had to struggle to make a living. And she told me that she knew from the beginning he would leave me eventually once we had children. She wasn't holding back!

I'll tell you, Roy was out of my studio in two seconds flat and said loudly, "Grandmother, I don't want to ever hear you say anything like that to my mother again. She's done a good job of it. And she is doing the best she can, and she doesn't need you goading her."

Another time, Roy said to her, "Grandmother, just because I'm young doesn't mean I don't know anything. And just because you're old doesn't mean you know everything."

Key #24: Loyalty is a two-way street.

So, Mother and Roy didn't get along well. He would speak his mind, and she didn't like it. I tried to be gentle with her and understand what she was going through, but her needling was wearisome at times. She would say some bizarre things. She would accuse me of lying to her. As I look back, I realize that people remember things in different ways, and she was probably just recalling whatever she was talking about differently than I did. But at the time, it was stressful.

Finally, one day I was so distraught over how difficult she was that I went to my minister and asked his advice. I didn't know how I could go on the way it was. The minister told me, "Hazel, you have allowed your Mother to bully you your entire life." I said that wasn't true; she was a good mother.

"No," he replied, "She was the same, but you didn't notice it until you crossed her. The first time you resisted her was when you got married. But she has been that way all along; you just didn't bear the brunt of it. You are the one that has let her do it, and now you have to be the one that stops her. I cannot say anything to her; she won't listen to me. You are the one that is going to have to stop her.

She's in your house now, and you are providing for her, cooking for her, taking her to the doctor. You are doing all these things for her, and if she doesn't appreciate that, you can tell her she can go live with someone else."

"I can't do that!" I replied.

"Hazel," he said, "you have allowed her to treat you like that. You are the only one that can make her quit. You have got to speak up for yourself."

I let out a deep breath and said to the minister, "Okay, tell me what I need to do. I have no idea what to say to her."

'I want you to sit down in front of her and say: "Mother, I brought you here to help take care of you, but I can see that you are not happy. So, I am going to provide you another place to live."

"I can't do that!" I repeated.

"Well, then you are going to have to put up with it because you are the only one who can stop it."

I thought it over and finally did what the preacher said. I set up a tape recorder to evidence the conversation we had. I didn't want Mother to misrepresent what we talked about to my brothers.

She went crazy. I told her, "You can stay here, but you are going to have to let me run my life. I am 58 years old, and you should not be trying to tell me what to do and how to live my life. So, if you want to stay here, you are going to have to learn to behave yourself." And she did!

Key #25: Do what you need to do to correct a bad situation. If you choose not to act, be prepared and content to put up with the results.

I can't say Mother turned around 180 degrees from that time on, but she tried harder, and we had some beautiful moments during the four years she stayed with me. We had season tickets for the symphony, which was lovely. We went to church, and she came with me to many musical events I attended. She still crocheted, and we started making handmade quilts together. I would cut out the quilt blocks, and she would sew the squares on the sewing machine.

I learned about the Grace quilting frame at a Piano Teachers conference in Salt Lake City. It allowed me to turn the quilt edges by myself rather than needing two people. While I kept that old frame Quentin had fashioned, I bought the Grace frame so that I wouldn't need another person's help. Now I was able to keep the fabric taut and tighten it more if needed. I could roll the finished part of the quilt up and work on the hard-to-reach middle pieces more comfortably. Despite painful arthritis and gnarled hands, Mother loved staying industrious by sewing those quilts.

When Mother turned 90 in 1988, we had a fantastic birthday party for her. It was the first birthday party she had ever had. Everyone was here: The friends she made here in Denver, both my brothers and their wives, all of Mother's grandchildren and even a great-great-grandchild or two. We let 90 balloons go up in the air in celebration of the occasion. It was a happy time.

Unfortunately, after her birthday, Mother had so many medical problems that I just couldn't keep working and be her nurse at the same time. I was wearing myself out trying to care for Mother, take her to doctor's appointments all the time, and maintain my piano teaching schedule. My brothers and I finally had to move her to a facility with more care. Just like deciding to have her come live with me, choosing to move her out was very difficult for me.

My brothers were against putting Mother in a nursing home. They wanted me to hire a nurse and keep her at home with me for a while longer. They told me that since I was the daughter in the family, it was my job to take care of Mother. Well, I had learned something over the years, and put my foot down and said no. I explained we had tried getting a nurse and it was next to impossible to get a qualified live in nurse. It would cost nearly as much as a nursing facility.

My brothers agreed to put Mother into an assisted living facility well north of where I live. I didn't think that was the answer, but they insisted that was all she needed. It took me 45 minutes one way to visit her, and I was expected to see her every day! It felt like I was reliving the same bad dream repeatedly.

I tried to visit Mother regularly, but in the first six weeks in the assisted living facility, she was in and out of the hospital all the time. The manager of the facility called me and told Mother she was not a candidate for assisted living and needed full-time nursing care. I told her to call my brothers. She did, and they finally moved her to a nursing care facility. About a year before she died, she started having congestive heart failure, and they moved her to nursing care in the lower altitude of San Antonio in hopes that the change of elevation would alleviate her condition.

Watching your parent age is no laughing matter, but I did get a chuckle one day when I got a call from my brother after Mother had moved back to Texas. The entire time Mother was here in Denver, I never heard a bad word about either of my brothers, only moaning and complaining about my offense of the day.

So, my brother called and said to me, "Aren't you the fair-haired one now?"

"Why?" I asked.

"Oh," he said, "Mother says everything was perfect at your house. Everything was wonderful. You took such better care of her than they do in the nursing home she is in."

I just laughed, and said to him "Ha! And she is in a home not in your house. Well multiply that tirade by about a thousand, and you'll understand how it was here!"

I couldn't help chuckling over that one. My brothers found out a little bit of what I went through.

Key #26: Making tough decisions for an aging parent is not easy for anyone. Seek advice from others, but let your heart make the final decision.

Mother died July 7, 1992, and she was 93 years old. Since then, my brothers and I have become very close. They started coming to my family reunions in 1998 and haven't missed one. My oldest brother, Harold, has since died, but James is now 90, and I plan to see him again this summer.

My mother and I often had a rocky relationship, but I learned a couple of valuable lessons through my experiences with her.

First, we need to show compassion to our parents. We live in a different world than they lived in and it's changing faster and faster all the time. That rapid change can be frightening, and despite your differences, I think you need to be gentle with them.

Key #27: Show compassion to people, even if you have differences with them.

And second, don't let yourself be victimized by someone even if they are close to you or an authority figure. My preacher helped me understand that I am the captain of my circumstances and that is a lesson that I will never forget again.

Key #28: You are the captain of your circumstances.

☐ .

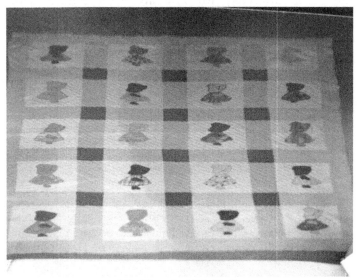

My Dutch Girl Quilt

CHAPTER 6: UNAFRAID: BEING WILLING TO FACE THE UNKNOWN

My second step to a Musical life (U) is about developing the mindset that you are the underwriter of your future. Yes, you will have challenges and problematic encounters, but despite it all, it is possible to remain unshaken.

There is another spoke to this step that is hard to put into words, and that is to have the disposition that is willing to face things that are new and, while exciting, a little scary to achieve your purpose. What is that unknown? It's different for everyone. You may fear the unknown of a new relationship, starting your own business or taking a trip. All these things can be intimidating. To make your future, you have to be willing to be unafraid in the face of the unknown.

About five years ago, I was still teaching piano at the age of 82 and didn't see an end in sight. I loved my students and their families. I enjoyed sharing my passion for music with the next generation. A part of me, however, was growing weary of the same old routine after so many years.

Around that same time a friend of mine, Ellie Newberry, who lived in Savannah, Georgia, introduced me to a nutritional supplement called Juice Plus. I was not ready to hear about it, that's for sure. I was very reluctant to try the product as she suggested. Ellie was persistent, and I began to realize that if I were going to continue life as I intended, I'd better start focusing on better nutrition.

I finally, reluctantly, tried the products. In only a few days, I suddenly realized I was regular for the first time in my life. I started noticing other positive changes in my physical and mental health. My hands were no longer cold all the time. I had more energy than I used to. I slept more soundly at night.

Some of my piano students seemed to be allergic to everything. I wondered if their nutrition could be what was wrong with them. Maybe their diets were not giving them all the nutrients they needed.

I shared Juice Plus with one of these students. He inspired his mother to try it, and within a month no longer needed to take his allergy medicine! His mother's cholesterol dropped, and she stopped getting the intense sugar cravings that she had before. Overall, both my student and his family started feeling much better both physically and mentally.

Well, after I told one person, I told another. And then I told somebody else. Pretty soon, the company was sending me money for my referrals!

When you go to a restaurant, and you love the food, what is the next thing you usually do? Don't you tell your friends? And when your friends go to the restaurant, does the restaurant pay you for sending them? Never.

If you see a movie that you love, do you tell people to see the film? And then the theatre sends you money, right? No, probably not.

But with Juice Plus, I would tell people about it and how it can change their lives by making them healthier. And the company sent me money.

Key #29: Some secrets are okay to tell others.

I tell people about Juice Plus, and if they subscribe to it, I get paid. It has been the most straightforward thing I have done in my life. And yet, for many, promoting their product or service can be one of the most challenging things in the world.

A former student of mine, Lacey, became a piano teacher and we have kept up with each other over the years. We were catching up on the phone one day, and she was grumbling about her students – how they will not practice and how hard she had to work. "Hazel," she said, "I am running myself ragged. And I'm not making enough money. I am just so frustrated."

I consoled her and then thought, why not? I guess I'll tell her about Juice Plus. So, I did, and she laughed and said, "Oh, Hazel, I've been taking Juice Plus for years!"

"I never heard about it from you! Why didn't you tell me about it?" I asked.

"Well, I'm a representative," she told me, "but I don't do anything with it. I just can't ask my students to buy from me."

"Boy, do you have it backwards, Lacey," I said. "You probably have students who have allergies or are sick a lot with colds. Why are you withholding this information from them? You owe it to them to tell them how healthy they could feel by taking Juice Plus. It's not right for you not to be telling them! Juice Plus is something that can help them."

Lacey didn't say much to me, but about two weeks later I received a call from her. "Hazel," she said, "You have been my mentor once again. I heard what you said and started sharing Juice Plus, and now I have so many customers that I am on the fast track to the next level in the organization."

At the next Juice Plus annual conference, at the time of this writing, Lacey will be given public recognition on stage for getting to the top level in the organization. My goal is to get there too one day. I may have initially mentored her, but now she is encouraging me!

Key #30: Selling anything is easy when you know how much it will help the person who needs it.

Juice Plus has taught me innumerable lessons about how to face the future unafraid. A little over a year ago, the company was opening its 26th national branch in Dubai. Dubai has a high incidence of Type Two Diabetes. Growing anything in Dubai is difficult because it is surrounded by sand. So, they have to import most of their food, which will naturally have a high content of processed sugar and salt. So, the citizens of Dubai desperately need proper nutrition. The King of the United Arab Emirates invited Juice Plus to come to Dubai to share our diet support.

The company wanted to have a big launch in Dubai in January 2017, and at the Saint Louis National Conference in the fall of 2016, they encouraged anyone who could attend the Grand Opening to travel there and participate. I had just won $2,000 at the wrap-up giveaway, based on business activity. Depending on what you have accomplished over a period, you get your name added more and more times. There are about 8,000 people's names in the pot, so to have a chance to win, you have to put in the work so that your name is added several times. I decided there was no better way to spend my winnings than to do this fun thing and go to Dubai.

The hotel in Dubai was the most luxurious hotel I have ever stayed. The bathrooms are made from marble. The workers in the hotel were terrific. They were finely dressed. I assured my children that I would not leave the hotel as they were afraid for my safety. When the conference was not in session, I spent my time talking to many of the hotel employees and shared my story about Juice Plus. They were all fascinated and excited that we were there. Only on the last day I was there did I find out that typical citizens of Dubai are not allowed to have credit cards. So, there was no way they could have bought Juice Plus.

We had 1,500 people at the conference, and very few were from the U.S. The audience was from Asia, Africa, India, Europe - from all over really. It was magnificent to see so many people from all over the world coming together in peace and unity to learn how to live a healthier and longer life.

Surprisingly, Dubai reminded me a lot of America. I expected all the women to be wearing burkas, but they were not. I see more burka-wearing Muslims walking the streets here in Colorado than those I saw while in Dubai. There were many wealthy people in attendance, but poor people as well.

Key #31: Don't judge a people by its place.

While I was there, I was asked to do some live videos to promote the launch and the Juice Plus products. Those videos led to an invitation by Loren Slocum-Lahav, a Juice Plus leader to a boot camp for her downline in Las Vegas Nevada. Loren told me that she wanted me to come as her guest and be part of an interview panel to encourage the older generation to get involved in Juice Plus. People think they are too old to start a new adventure by the time they are 60 or 70 years old. I was 86 when I attended her boot camp. It was such an outstanding event and went so well that I am going back again this year.

Juice Plus ended up being a delightful surprise in my life both as a vehicle for personal growth and financial stability. After about two years promoting Juice Plus, I realized I didn't have the time or the need to teach piano anymore. I decided I would rather retire after 74 years of teaching and pursue Juice Plus full-time.

Key #32: Things have a way of working out the way they are supposed to. Be open to opportunities, and you'll be surprised at what happens.

It's funny, though. When Ellie first approached me to try the Juice Plus products, I never intended to pursue it as a business, ever. I told myself I was too cool, too organized, and already set in my daily routine. Looking back, however, I think I was fearful, just as Lacey was, to offend people by talking with them about what others might judge as a questionable pyramid scheme.

I soon discovered that my fears were unfounded. Talking about Juice Plus to people I knew, or strangers alike, happened so naturally. As more people got involved with it, the more excited I became. I decided at that point that helping people to improve their health is the way I want to spend the rest of my life. One of my typical sayings in conversation is, "I want to help people be healthy, and wealthy if they want to be."

Too many people today do not have enough money and have resigned themselves to never being financially stable. For the first 80 years of my life, I too shared in that circumstance. Now, I have more time and money than I've ever had in my life! And, working the business is the most natural thing I've ever done.

Key #33: Embrace your desires and go for it, unafraid.

CHAPTER 7: SET YOURSELF UP FOR SUCCESS

Becoming the underwriter of your life means more than taking charge of and commanding your future. It's more than acting unafraid and unshaken by the obstacles you are bound to encounter. It also means setting yourself up for success.

Setting yourself up for success can be an intimidating endeavor because it is hard to know where to start. Everyone has a different opinion as to what you should do, evidenced by the thousands and thousands of self-help and business success books on the market. I do not claim to be an expert, but over the years I have come to find that two things are crucial to ensure that I am prepared, physically and mentally, to act and succeed at my goals. Those two things are good health and the support of family.

Health

When I was twenty years old, I lost my first baby to toxemia (preeclampsia). I went into labor on my due date and thought everything was going according to plan. In those days, mothers in labor were given ether during the birth, which is horrible stuff. I never knew anything about the delivery because I was unconscious for the entire time. It was a natural childbirth, but apparently, my blood pressure was too high, and they kept me sedated for three days because of concern that I would have a stroke. Quentin and his family had a funeral for the baby, but I was still in the hospital under sedation. I never had the chance to say a proper goodbye.

It was my first baby, and I was only twenty years old and knew nothing about the whole process. When they finally sent me home, and my milk came in, I was in horrible pain and didn't know how to help it. Thank goodness for my mother-in-law who was a nurse and explained to me what had happened and what to do.

We had not planned to have children right away, and when I found out I was pregnant, I was devastated. I felt foolish and naïve when it happened so quickly. When the baby died, it felt like God was punishing me by taking it away from me. And after it happened, the doctor told me I probably couldn't have any more children, and it was better if I didn't try. I was horrified. It was a terrible time for me.

I grew skinny and started having pain in my side, near my kidney. The doctor said my kidney had dropped and they needed to take it out. My mother-in-law stopped that pretty quickly!

You know, I think some people just let the doctors do whatever they want. A doctor will say this is what has to be done, and so you say okay, go ahead. I learned you could ask questions and learn the alternatives. But I wouldn't have been that smart if my mother-in-law was not there to educate me.

I lost a lot of confidence in doctors from those two experiences. My whole life I have tried to be more self-reliant when it comes to my health than most people seem to be. I didn't take my children to the doctor every time they sniffled; I always tried more holistic care than just taking them to the doctor for medication.

As I get older, I know plenty of people who are pals with their doctor; it's as if they see them daily. And they will take anything a doctor prescribes with no independent research.

When Mother came to live with me, I discovered how harmful medicines are to our bodies. Drugs have different chemicals that our bodies do not know how to handle. For example, Mother would have pain from arthritis, and the drugs they gave her to ease her suffering would upset her stomach. So, they would give her medicine to calm her upset stomach, and that would agitate something else.

Your doctor is not a god, and you do not have to believe everything a doctor tells you. Yes, we need doctors, but generally, they have been taught to diagnose, remove and prescribe. I think that prevention should be the primary goal, not finding a solution after an illness has already taken hold of you.

Key #34: Prevention is better than cure. Don't blindly rely on your doctor to make you healthy.

After I saw Mother deal with all the problems with her medications, I decided I'm not going to take medication unless and until I absolutely have to. Medication does nothing but aggravate other issues. And they have so many side effects that I don't want to be part of. I want to stay healthy. So, I'm going to do the best I can to stay healthy. I'm 88 years old at the time of this writing. So far, so good!

I'm living proof that you do not have to expect to slow down as you age. Through time and repetition, you and I have been conditioned to accept the prevailing belief that as you get older, you start to have more health conditions. As a result, your quality of life will naturally decrease. I don't even give it a thought myself, even at my age. I am on the go from morning to night and can sleep well and get up and start all over again.

As a medical doctor, Dr. Paul Williams, one of my direct up-line, has been one of the early medical proponents of Juice Plus and advocates prevention over cure. I have learned so much from him, as well as from Dr. William Sears, who I studied with to receive my Certified Health Coach diploma. Dr. Sears claims that 75% of all chronic disease is preventable. That is my aim, prevention. An ounce of prevention is worth a pound of cure. If I can avoid getting sick, that is naturally a lot easier than getting ill and having to get well.

A lot of people aren't willing to be self-reliant about their health and commit to the nutrition and exercise it takes to prevent illness. That's sad because it doesn't take much.

When I was 52, my youngest son, Roy, was a physical training coach for ROTC while he attended Metro State University in Denver. He was a triathlete and won several sports awards in high school. He was a "jock" in every sense of the word. Roy was living with me at home while he attended school, and one Sunday, Roy took me to church. After the sermon, I stood up, and my knees cracked so loud that you could have heard them two rows away! Roy leaned over to me and said, "What was that? Was that your knees cracking like that? Was that you?" I didn't even notice my knees cracking.

On our way home, he said, "I'm going to put you on an exercise routine. I'm not going to let this happen to you." I had never been on an exercise routine or paid much attention to formal exercise programs, but I always did try to keep my weight down. Roy said, "I want you to do 40 pushups, 40 sit-ups, and 40 deep knee bends, and ten more minutes of cardio for a 20-minute workout. And, I want you to do it every day, not three days a week, not five days a week, every day, seven-days-a-week, you will be able to do those same 40 pushups, sit-ups, and deep knee-bends when you're 80."

"40 pushups!" I said. "I can't even do one pushup!" He replied, "Start with one and keep adding one every day as

you're able and pretty soon you'll be able to do 40 in a row."
He was right, and it didn't take long. I've been doing that
exercise routine ever since. It doesn't cost anything. It doesn't
take much time. If you adopt this routine for yourself and do
the same exercises every single day, seven days a week, you too
will be in better shape than any of your friends that are ten
years younger than you are when you get to your aging years.

Roy watched me exercise for a few days to make sure I was
doing the pushups correctly, but then he never brought up the
subject again. He didn't need to. From the day I started Roy's
exercise routine, I had a strong desire to stay healthy, and I can
still do all of those exercises today. Whenever I'm called up on
stage, people who have seen me speak before expect to see me
do some pushups. For those seeing me for the first time, the
surprised look on their faces is priceless. I called Roy after I
turned 80 and said, "Thank you! You saved my life! I would
have never done those exercises unless it was you telling me to
do them."

I eat healthily and continue daily to take Juice Plus products to
supplement what I cannot get from my food. It's not
complicated, anyone can do it, and it has improved the quality
of my life.

Our health is our wealth. I don't care how much money you
have. If you do not have good health, you still are broke. And
if you have good health, you don't have to have tons of money
because you can always work.

**Key #35: Your health is your wealth. Adopt an
exercise program from someone you trust and do it
every day.**

Family

As important as our health is, our family is even more critical to our success. I've learned this lesson from good experiences and bad throughout my life. We spend more time with our family over the course of a lifetime than with anybody else. Of course, how those relationships hold up is essential to achieving your purpose!

Spouses/Partners

My Aunt Lorene told me when I was a little girl that I should never marry anyone for financial reasons rather than love. I have seen many women do that, especially after their first husband dies or leaves. The first thing they want to do is to find someone to take care of them. After my first husband, Quentin left our family, I vowed to never again enter another toxic relationship. I don't want to be treated as an inferior or subservient ever again. Been there. Done that. And what did it get me? Five beautiful children and thick skin, but not much else!

Key #36: Never allow someone to make you go crazy just because they are.

I will be sharing much more of my times with Quentin later as we get further along in the M.U.S.I.C. process for life. I learned a great deal about self-esteem and determination from my time as Quentin's wife. Looking back, I think Quentin misinterpreted the Bible's teaching about a woman's family role. That caused an irreparable rift. God made Eve out of the rib of man. She did not come from the dirt of the ground as Adam did. God created Eve to be his helpmate. He made her to be at Adam's side. That's why he took the bone that he made Eve out of from his side - not from his head for him to be lording over her, or from his feet so he could kick her around. A woman is supposed to be man's helpmate, at his side. I fully believe that. And I lived it. I did it. Quentin saw my role more submissively.

It took a long time to realize that my relationship with Quentin was atypical and harmful. It wasn't until I met and married my second husband, Buddy Ramsbotham that I realized how God's plan for a man and his wife could work so perfectly together. Buddy was 65 when we met, and he quickly became the love of my life. He was the one who made me realize that I could do anything that I wanted. He was so supportive of me about everything that I wanted to do, without feeling inferior himself. We brought out the best in each other, which is the way God intended marriage to work.

Today's culture suggests that a man and woman should remain self-sufficient despite being married to each other. In my experience, that approach makes men leery of doing the wrong thing and woman continually unhappy. God created man to protect and woman to nurture. There are many ways to make that plan work, but primarily, a couple should follow God's directions in their partnership.

If you are struggling in your relationship, I urge you to meditate on God's directions and ask Him for help. God will guide you in ways that you never thought of or noticed before. Don't try to solve every controversy on your own.

Key #37: Meditate on God's directions and ask Him for help.

Children

They say, "The family that plays together stays together." Music has always been a significant chord in my life, and I needed my children to appreciate its rare qualities as much as I did. I always said that I wanted my children to love God first, music second, and hoped they would love me when it was all over.

Every one of my children could play multiple instruments. Of course, they all played piano, but in addition to that, Roma had a clarinet, Randy had a French horn, Roy a trombone, Ronda an oboe and Ree a flute. Our family also had a string bass, which Randy, especially, played well, and a drum set.

Some of my fondest family memories before Quentin left were those in our family band. We first performed in public when my eldest, Roma was 11 and her brother, Randy was 9. Roma played the piano and Randy the string bass. I was on the accordion, and Quentin sang and played guitar. We would perform at banquets and weddings and all sorts of events all over the county.

Ronda (3) and the twins Roy and Ree (2) were too little to join, at first, but we would bring them along, and they would sit up on the stage with us and perform a piece or two even at their young age. Ronda would sing a solo by herself. Then, the twins would sing Put Your Arms Around Me Honey, which was a popular tune when I was growing up. They did little actions to match the words of the song, and it was adorable. Those little kids were a big hit with the crowd.

I remember one night someone in the audience yelled out, "Put the babies up where we can see them!" I stood them up on a table. They were too young at the time to be performing yet when this happened. They just stood up on the table. After the show, Randy, who played the string bass all night, moaned, "It isn't fair! They get as much applause as I do for one tune, and I'm working all night!"

You might have noticed that all five of my children (Roma, Randy, Ronda, Roy, and Ree) have names beginning with the letter "R." Their middle names also began with R and, of course, Roberts starts with an R as well. The three youngest children started performing as the Triple R Trio when the twins were 5years-old and continued singing together until they were in their teens. They won the Stars of Tomorrow contest held by the Kiwanis Club more times than I can remember over the years, and one time performed the song Who will Buy? from the Musical Oliver. That song was such a hit that the Triple R Trio was asked to perform it multiple times over the years. To me, however, their most memorable performance was when the Triple R Trio provided all of the music for my oldest son Randy's wedding. I was so proud of my whole family that day.

We played together as a band right up until Quentin left the family. We had family music night every Tuesday night. That is when we rehearsed. Quentin's idea of rehearsing was nebulous – he wanted to play something two times and move onto something else. I tried to explain to him that children needed more rehearsal than a couple of times through the song. The twins, especially, seemed to make a lot of mistakes during our rehearsal, but it was eerie. During their performance, they always performed it flawlessly. I was always so nervous before they performed. I would sit there thinking oh no, this is the part they didn't get in rehearsal, but then they would get through it without a hitch.

You can't very well be proud of your family unless you are close enough to them to know them. Lots of families are not close. Often, people tell me that they do not want to be around their family or that they don't care anything about their family. I think families are essential. After all, we are flesh and blood, and we should get along.

Key #38: Your family is your greatest blessing.

I told my kids I loved them every day of their lives and that I was proud of them. If I am not willing to stand up for them, who would? I did not excuse them when they did something wrong. And, it was a firm rule that if they got in trouble at school, they were in trouble at home. I was very strict with them, but I told them that I loved them because they were mine. They knew that I would love them no matter what. But I also taught them that no one else would like them unless they behaved. I made them behave because I wanted the whole world to love my children.

The most misquoted and misused verse in the Bible could be, "Judge Not." Society stops at that and interprets it to mean that we shouldn't discipline or set a moral code for our children. But, consider the rest of the verse:

Do not judge others. For you will be treated as you treat others. The standard you use in judging is the standard by which you will be judged. (Matthew 7: 1-2)

The message is clearly that you will be evaluated with the same standard as you evaluate. In other words, be firm but fair.

Key #39: Your family needs you to be firm, but fair.

If you think about it, we judge things all the time. We judge what we are going to eat or wear, or where we are going to go. But people have turned it around to say you can't discipline at all. Now everybody is afraid to say anything about another's behavior and our children are not being taught to obey their parents. In my belief, that's the beginning of anarchy. Because when children are not trained to obey their parents, they don't obey their teachers or any other authority figures.

The essential point is that it is our responsibility as parents to set our kids up for success by teaching them how to behave in society. Schools can't do it. They are over-regulated and subject to too many restrictions to count anymore. It is the parent's responsibility. Assign your children chores. Check up on them to make sure their schoolwork is getting done. Encourage them to do extra activities such as music or sports. Be prepared to discipline, when needed, in a firm but loving way. Start early, so that your children grow up believing it to be normal. Because it should be normal!

I'm not saying my children were perfect. Don't get me wrong; they were not perfect in their growing up years.

With five children, I was always breaking up battles among them. I didn't allow them to fight with each other. I told them to be thankful they had a brother or sister and would not allow bickering. Bickering is just a habit. I just tried to teach them to love and care about each other rather than to fight each other.

Key # 40: You can foster the habit of your children getting along with each other and being happy with each other, or you can instill the habit of constant fighting. Which will it be?

Tranquil family life is essential for you as parents as much as it is for your children. A house in chaos has no positive contribution to the fulfillment of your purpose in life. Children are supposed to come and share your life. Enrich your life. They aren't supposed to run your life.

The best advice I can offer is to start with kind, loving discipline early. That cute toddler climbing up on the coffee table will not be so cute in five years. Set the boundaries early, gently and kindly.

Key #41: The inmates don't run the asylum. Run your family the same way.

Many older parents find themselves "helping" their adult children out repeatedly. I hear it all the time – parents sending money because of car trouble, or a broken furnace or any number of things. No parent wants to see their child suffer, that's why they help them. But it can strain the family relationship if an adult child comes back for help over and over, especially for a parent on a fixed income.

What is my advice for young parents? Rather than give your children everything they ask for, teach them early to be self-sufficient. Doing that will provide them with the skills they need to be on their own and be able to take care of their problems before they happen.

I had little choice in the matter; I struggled financially during most of my children's growing up years. Thank the Lord I am so much better off financially today. But back then, we were always broke. If Quentin hadn't left and we had enough money that the kids felt comfortable in asking for help, I may have thought differently too. But as it was, my children learned early on that they couldn't ask me for money because I was struggling to make it on my own. So, they just dealt with money matters by themselves. Looking at how they turned out today, I see how that helped build self-reliant, responsible adults, and I am so proud of them all.

Key #42: "Happiness belongs to the self-sufficient." - Aristotle

M.U.S.I.C.
PART 3: S
STUDENT – SEARCHING - SPIRITEDLY

Work toward your purpose as a **Student** would, while staying open and receptive to all people and opportunities that come your way. God may provide you avenues to achieve your purpose, which you would never get on your own. Only by **Spiritedly Searching** for what others can contribute will you reach your highest potential.

Hazel & Buddy

CHAPTER 8: MY BUDDY HUSBAND

After my first husband, Quentin, left the family, I accepted that I was never going to marry again. I never expected to marry again. In fact, I didn't want to marry again. Aunt Lorene had told me to never marry for economic reasons, and that lesson stuck with me. So, I knew I had to be able to make it on my own before I married someone. I was not going to be dependent on anybody else to make a living again. Those days were over; I never wanted to be in that kind of situation.

I wasn't searching for a husband.

The truth is, when I first married Quentin, I didn't know very much about men. I thought I did because I had three older brothers, but I didn't understand anything about how men think. So, I was very trusting. But after my first marriage, oh boy, that's when all of that changed! Even though we stayed married from 1949 until 1977, Quentin had checked out of the family by 1965. It felt like I was living with a stranger. He just got increasingly distant. So, for almost 25 years, I was alone.

My method for coping after the divorce was to keep my head down and work hard. I never expected to meet another man that I would fall in love with and want to spend the rest of my life with. I didn't trust men and grew to believe there were no good men in existence. It took me a long time to realize that there are some good men out there. When a good man finally did enter my life, I was surprised that I could trust a man again.

Key #43: Accept the unexpected. It can bring happiness even if you are not looking for it.

I first met Buddy in January 1990, and I was just a kid at age 60. A friend of mine got me interested in square dancing lessons, but since I didn't know many people except the parents of my piano students and the members of my church, I didn't know where I would find a partner. My friend said, "You do not need a partner for square dancing because the instructors will provide them in class."

At my first lesson, I found out what she meant. They had what they called Square Dance Angels, who were seasoned square dancers who went to the classes to have fun and to help people to learn.

Buddy was a Square Dance Angel, and after the first class, we seemed to get paired up over and over again. I didn't realize it until he told me later, but Buddy was not letting anyone else be my partner! Occasionally, when we had a break, we would visit and talk a little bit, but that was as far as it went for a long time.

In March of that year, the remains of my brother, Charles, were returned to the family from Vietnam where he died in battle serving our country. I will be sharing more of Charles' story in a later Chapter. But I went to Arlington National Cemetery for his military funeral. I missed a couple of square dancing classes, and when I returned, Buddy was taken aback to see me. Apparently, it was pretty typical for someone to miss a couple of weeks and then never return. Buddy was surprised and pleased I came back!

From then on, we became more talkative and friendly. Finally, in June we exchanged phone numbers. Buddy was very good looking. He dressed impeccably, didn't smoke, drink or swear (well, at least in front of me). And Buddy was a modest, decent man. I'm not sure how he stayed so pure for 65 years before he met me!

Buddy made me feel like I could do anything, and I filled a hole in his life that he had suffered with since he served in World War II. He was a medic in the first line of defense to take the Philippines back from the Japanese. The horror of the war left him with PTSD and he never fully recovered.

Buddy was 65 when we met and had never married. He didn't think he was marrying material. It wasn't until I met him that he began to open and tell about what happened in the war. We started out as friends that never intended to marry, each for our reasons, but our relationship developed rapidly into a romance. We were married on September 30, 1990 and were together ten and a half years. He was the love of my life.

Even Mother liked Buddy! She had just moved near my brothers to nursing care when I met him, so one of the first trips we made together was down to Texas to meet her. She had had such a fit about me marrying Quentin that I was anxious about how the introduction might go. My first inclination was to try to protect him but then I figured he could take care of himself.

Mother was so happy for us! It was entirely different from the way she had been when I got married the first time. I just stood there with my mouth hanging open. I guess she was concerned that I had been alone for so long, and she was thrilled I had found someone. Her only question was, "How long was it between the time you decided to get married until you actually did get married?" Buddy answered, "We've known each other about nine months, but when we finally decided to get married, it was a Wednesday, and we got married the following Sunday."

I held my breath because that was nearly the same thing that happened the first time around too. I told Mother on a Wednesday that Quentin and I were getting married, and then we married the next Sunday. She sure wasn't pleased about it then.

But all Mother said was, "That's better than I did! When I left my house that morning, I didn't expect to be getting married that night." I was so surprised at her reaction. Mother was entirely different from the way she had been when I got married the first time. She must have sensed that Buddy and I were soul mates.

Key #44: People can't change time but time changes people.

Buddy didn't like the name Hazel because it was too similar to Hazael, a bad guy in the Old Testament (1st King 19, verse 15). So, he started calling me Becky, for Rebecca in the Bible, which was fine with me because I always hated the name Hazel. My grandchildren still call me Grandma Becky, and they don't even know why. But some of my children did not approve. They didn't think Buddy had the right to change my name. The others asked, "What does it matter? She's still Mom to us. We aren't going to call her that name anyway. She is just Mom so what do you care?" I tried to get other people to call me Becky, but they would not. I finally gave up after Buddy passed away and went back to Hazel. But there are still people who met me during that time that call me nothing but Becky.

Buddy and my children loved each other too. The kids were thrilled that he had never been married with children because they did not want to share me with his children. But they were all glad to see me with someone that made me happy. Buddy was so very kind. He treated me like a queen.

Buddy died of a stroke January 20, 2001. We were together for nearly 11 years. He was a retired stonemason, but I was still teaching piano full-time and very busy at that. I did not have a lot of time to do other things. We kept on square dancing and loved it! I made us matching outfits, a shirt for him and a dress for me, and we went square dancing once a week or so.

We made time for travel, which became increasingly important and enjoyable to us both. Once I received flying privileges from my son Roy, the commercial pilot, we would fly everywhere together. The last trip we took together was to London, England. Buddy was getting increasingly feeble by then, and that was one place he wanted to go. During the War, there was a favorite song called the White Cliffs of Dover. So, we wanted to see the White Cliffs of Dover. We were gone for a fantastic two weeks.

Buddy's last name, Ramsbotham, is a common English name and we went to Ramsbotham, the town. To get there from London, we had to take the subway, then another train, and a bus, until we finally arrived. It was so hard to find how to get there. Ramsbotham was not a well-known place. But we played like we were detectives and hunted it down. We learned a lot about the town's history. We discovered that Ramsbotham is the town where Robert Peale lived, and he started the police organization in England. That is the reason that England policemen are called Bobbies. There is a large monument for Robert Peale in Ramsbotham. And I have a charm bracelet that has the monument of Robert Peale on it.

Key #45: Travel nurtures an adventuresome spirit. Better to see something than to just hear or read about it.

I am so glad I was open-minded enough to welcome Buddy into my life after 25 years of being alone. It was a different world for me. We were born in the same era and from similar backgrounds. We knew all the same songs and historical events from when we were growing up. We knew each other so well; we could finish each other's sentences. We seemed to agree on everything and rarely bickered. It was just so lovely to have someone so compatible to spend my time.

It was a fulfilling and sweet period in my history. I would tell Buddy how much more fun he made my life and he would reply, "You made my life. I didn't have one before you." It was very romantic. My friends would always ask if he had a brother!

I never had that kind of companionship before. And Buddy was a companion. He was in my corner for everything. He was a real buddy, and that's why I call him my Buddy husband.

Key #46: Even if you aren't searching for something, be ready to welcome it into your life when it finds you.

CHAPTER 9: LIVE, LEARN, AND GO ON

Part of being a lifelong student involves finding the lessons in not so pleasant situations. One such experience I encountered had to do with learning that people can change, seemingly at the drop of a hat.

Not long after Mother came to live with me in Denver, June became a long-term renter in my home. June was eight years older than I was. She was a member of the Mormon Church. June was originally from Canada and a member of the Royal Air Force. She met and married a fellow soldier in her youth. The man had received orders that he would be leaving for England within a week's time. June wanted to get pregnant immediately and have a baby, although her husband didn't think it was the right time. She was dead set on having a baby. In those days, women had the mindset that they should have a baby before their husband went off to war. If the husband was to die in battle, they figured, a baby would carry on the spirit and family name of the deceased. Most people felt that way at the time.

A baby is what June wanted. Her husband did not. But, in the short time they were together as a married couple, June became pregnant. He went off to war, and June's daughter was born while he was overseas. He did not know anything about the baby. In World War II, men went for the duration. They did not have furloughs after 6 or 8 months or tour periods as they do now. When the war ended, and he came home, he discovered a three-year-old child in his house! It didn't go well, and they split up.

Key # 47: Honesty brings honor to those you love.

June spent the rest of her life marrying men to provide a father for her daughter. She married five times, and her daughter grew increasingly rebellious. June was a grandma by the time her daughter was 15 years old.

June helped her daughter raise the first baby, but by the time I met her, June's daughter had never married and had five children. June was in a hole financially because her daughter and grandchildren would freeload off her continuously. When June finally couldn't pay her bills anymore, she knew she needed to get help.

June sought the advice of the local Bishop of the Mormon Church, whose seven children had all studied piano with me. He knew that I had spare rooms that I let occasionally, and he asked if I would be willing to rent to June so that her daughter could no longer come and sponge off of her.

Key #48: Connect with others, and they will send opportunity your way.

June moved in and from the first was like the sister that I never had. I just loved her. She was an excellent help with Mother. June loved the arrangement too. After about a year, she told me she had never had such a tranquil life as when she was living in my house. June was so surprised that I was so even-keeled. Never would my emotions flare up one moment and down in the dumps the next.

June was a bit scatterbrained and was always doing something silly that she thought I would kick her out over. For example, I had asked her to water my petunias while I was gone. The petunias were in a pot, so I explained they just needed a little bit of water. When I returned, the flowers were dead and the roots exposed. She had just let the water run forever and ever in the pots.

Another time, I had replaced the carpet in her room in the basement, and she was refilling her waterbed. I left to go to the store, and when I returned, the whole basement had flooded. She had gotten distracted by the phone and forgotten to turn it off. We had to clean up the entire basement from the water damage.

Then, there was the time that my son, Roy, got a purebred Dalmatian dog. He named her Janess. The dog was in heat and had two more days in her cycle until we were home free. I left to go to church on Sunday morning, and there was a foot of snow on the ground. I told June to keep the dog inside until I returned. When I got back from church Janess was nowhere to be found. June said she was whining to go out, so she let her out.

Well, the dog didn't come when called, so I got my boots on and trekked around until I found her behind the garage with another dog. Janess got pregnant resulting from that random encounter and gave birth to seven puppies. Roy and I suddenly found ourselves with seven mongrel puppies to raise and find homes for.

Every time June did one of these crazy things she was sure I would kick her out. I didn't because, despite her eccentric ways, I felt very close to her. But then, our relationship suddenly changed.

After Mother's escalating medical challenges inspired my brothers in Texas to move her closer to them, I filled her room by hosting foreign exchange students in my home. June would get friendly with the students and then try to convert them to Mormonism. That was not something I could allow, because the students were under my supervision, and the rules stated a host family could not do any more than invite foreign exchange students to church. Trying to change their core beliefs without their consent was forbidden.

June got very upset at me about that and started undermining me. She soon moved out of my home into the house of another Mormon couple. After June had moved out, one of the students I was hosting moved out of my home and in with June and the couple. They fraudulently told the foreign exchange organization that the student was related to the wife of the couple. When the student moved, I was forced to forfeit the $300 monthly fee I received for hosting. It was the craziest thing.

But the lunacy didn't end there. A former student whom I hosted while June was still living with me came to America for a visit from Japan. She stayed with me for a couple of nights but asked about June, and decided to spend the night, and the man came over to my place to get some clothes for her. I wasn't home at the time, and my current tenants in the basement did not know who he was. So, they refused to let him in until they could check with me.

Well, rather than wait for me to get home, June and these other folks called the police. When I returned that night, the police had come into my house without my knowledge and consent and went into the bedroom where the girl had been staying to get her things. I was astounded. I would have been more than happy to let them in if they would have waited until I was home.

When I called June on the phone, she hung up on me. So, I went over to their house, and they accused me of trying to steal my visitor's traveler's checks! Of course, I had not committed that offense. I didn't know the exchange student even had any money and would never go through her things.

It was the craziest thing that had ever happened to me. I was so hurt. I had done nothing but give June my love, my attention, and even my house for five years. And I thought she was a loyal friend. Her turning on me like that almost destroyed me. I was so upset.

Key #49: Even people you trust can be unpredictable. Trust your instinct, but with a watchful eye.

Sometimes, I just cannot figure out people very well. Whatever people tell me, I believe. It doesn't register with me that people might purposely lie to benefit their position somehow. June had been in my home for five years, and I thought she was trustworthy. I suppose it comes down to the love of money as being the root of all evil. I guess the $300 foreign exchange fee and the traveler's checks were enough incentive for her to ruin our relationship. It was a disappointing experience. I thought I would never have anyone beyond family live at my house again. I thought I had learned my lesson.

But, part of being a spirited searcher in life is to be willing to accept when God has other plans.

I married Buddy shortly after June moved out, and we didn't have any tenants in the house during the eleven years we were married. After he died, I had people stay with me in my house, but they were either family or very close friends of the family.

Then, Bill came along.

A friend of mine asked me about eleven years ago if I would rent out my basement to someone he knew. I told him, "No, because I don't have an outside entrance and anyone who rents it would have the run of the house." I didn't trust anyone to be in my home anymore.

He persisted and told me all about Bill, a close friend of his.

Bill was a truck driver. He had rented a room from a couple for six years and was looking for a similar arrangement. Bill didn't want to rent a whole apartment because he was on the road so often. But he did want a place to call home. My friend told me that Bill was sincere and trustworthy. We talked about it, but I didn't say yes right away.

After several persistent conversations with my friend, he brought Bill over to my house. I don't remember ever saying Bill could live here before or during that in-person meeting. But next thing I knew, he was moving in. And Bill has lived in my basement ever since.

My children were very concerned when he moved in. But I think the Lord has blessed me in this situation. Bill is a treasure. He is very quiet and makes no noise. Bill is very respectful of me when I have company and never comes upstairs to interrupt. And it has been a gift that he has taken over things that need to be done around here that I cannot handle on my own.

For example, I recently had insulation blown into the attic. When I came home, the contractor wanted payment. Bill investigated the attic with a flashlight, and they hadn't blown insulation beyond a short point in the attic. The contractor had left the whole back of the attic uninsulated. Bill called them on it, and they tried to use the excuse that their hose didn't reach that far. Bill directed them to where they could move their truck and get in through the garage. I would have never even thought to inspect their work like that. I told Bill, "You can never leave!"

Every time I think about it, I'm amazed that I have once again accomplished the three things in life I never thought I would experience again: A good man, one that I trust, and someone I'm willing to let live in my house. I cannot imagine running my home without Bill living there now. He is worth his weight in gold.

Key # 50: Even if you've been burned many times, someone will always come along to provide an improved situation, if you are open to it.

CHAPTER 10: LESSONS
FROM MY VISITORS

I mentioned in the last Chapter that I hosted foreign exchange students. As usual, there is more to that story!

My neighbor across the street was the one who asked me in 1983 if I would like to host foreign exchange students. "Heaven's no!" I replied, "I'm having enough trouble making ends meet as it is. I don't need to feed anyone else!"

He laughed and explained, no, these are the students that pay you to stay with you.

I said to him, okay, tell me more!

He told me about Bridge International School, an organization that was always looking for American hosts to house students from foreign countries. All you needed to do was speak English to the students, provide a place for them to stay and food. You were not required to cook the meals, just to have food available in the house. They paid $300 a month per student. Count me in!

I hosted approximately ten students over the years, from Malaysia, Guatemala, Columbia, and Japan. I hosted two students at a time. They would stay anywhere from a month to several months. Most of my guests were incredible. I can only remember telling one student to leave.

That particular student was from Japan, and he was very

spoiled. When he arrived on move-in day, he walked into the guest bedroom where he was to stay, and pointed at the bed and said, "This has to go." Then, he pointed at the armoire in the room and said, "This has to go too."

I replied earnestly, "No, none of this is going anywhere." He said he just wanted to sleep on the floor. I told him that he could sleep on the floor if he wanted, but I would not move the furniture out. He did not like that. But he came here to assimilate into the American lifestyle. I told him if that wasn't what he wanted, he could go back to Japan. I wasn't having him push me around.

As soon as he arrived, he started getting big care packages from his folks. It must have cost them a fortune to mail them. He stayed for about a week and was very rude to me. I had five children, and I never allowed them to talk to me in the manner and tone he delivered. I would have never put up with it. So, I told him to leave. But he was the only student who was a problem. All the rest of the students were fabulous.

Key # 51: Be brave enough to stand your ground when you need to.

I loved hosting the exchange students. They were very respectful. I cooked for them, and they liked the food. There was a Malaysian girl named Lily who enjoyed cooking. She offered to cook for me anytime I wanted to have a party. She was fantastic.

Ricardo was from Bogota, Columbia and was just darling. He called me "Mom" from the minute he got here. Ricardo was polite and easy to get along with. He first came in September or October and confided in me that Bogota could get cold.
"How cold are we talking?" I asked. Ricardo told me it could get as cold as fifty degrees. I laughed and said, "oh, are you ever in for a rude awakening here in Colorado!"

I didn't know that central heat was not available in Columbia where he grew up. I asked him one time what they do when it gets cold, and he replied, "Oh, we just wait until it gets warm." I thought that was the strangest thing to say! But I learned that while some homes have a fireplace, most have no heat source at all. So, when it gets cold, they just wrap-up in more clothes until it warms up. They just waited for it to get warm!

Ricardo would open his window about a foot wide every night. I would walk by his room in the morning and feel the cold air and close the window. I told him that I could not have him leaving that window open because I couldn't afford to heat the whole outside. "Heat?" Ricardo said, "What do you mean heat?" I tried to explain to him how furnaces worked, but he kept opening his window every night, and I kept closing it every morning.

My exchange students' stories made me realize how very fortunate we are in America, and how very spoiled. People who have never seen another way of living, think that having hot and cold water, indoor toilets, and heat is essential to survival. But, many other countries do not provide all those luxuries to everyone. I thank the Lord every day for being able to live in this wonderful country.

Key #52: Be thankful for where you live and for what you have. There is always someone who would love to have what you have.

Moriah is another young student that shared my home in 2012. She and her family lived in Washington State, and Moriah wanted to move to Denver to go to Phlebotomy School. I imagine she could have attended Phlebotomy school in Washington, but she wanted to spread her wings and leave home for a little while.

She came from a Christian family and, rather than seek out an apartment for Moriah to stay in, her parents called my church's office and asked if there was anyone who could let her live in their home while she attended school. I decided that since I had three daughters of my own and would have loved to have someone look out for them in the same situation, this was something I should do.

Moriah and her mother drove here in Moriah 's car, and her mother flew home after the weekend. I was prepared to lay down the law; no guys, no late parties, no drinking no smoking, the whole list. But we never even talked about it because she was so sweet and innocent. I didn't worry about it at all and did not need to.

Moriah's schooling was only on a part-time level, so Moriah tried to find a job. She wound up with a few temporary and part-time jobs, but none of them had enough hours to keep her busy. Moriah finally found a job as a delivery person for Blackjack Pizza. She never thought she would like it, but it ended up being an excellent fit for Moriah. She had a charming and sweet personality and was easy on the eyes. So, she got lots of tips. It didn't bother her one bit to be driving around all over town and delivering pizza, although I was a little concerned for her safety. Fortunately, Moriah never worked late at night and had a GPS in her car to find where she needed to go. The job worked out well for her.

As it turned out, Moriah did not pass the phlebotomy course the first time through, so she had to wait to attend the class again. Two times a charm, she passed the second time. But then, she had to wait to be placed into a clinical internship, which was required to complete the course. Moriah ended up staying in my home much longer than we all initially intended.

Moriah and I grew very close. I taught her how to cook, and we did a lot of things together. Having her in my life was fun because I would suggest doing something spontaneously, and

Moriah would agree in a flash. I missed her when she was gone. We had a wonderful time.

Moriah's parents were appreciative of me, not that I did anything particularly special to mold and shape Moriah. She just lived with me, and we got along well. I felt like I benefited from her visit. She was just a darling. That surprised her parents! They told me how stubborn Moriah had been at home and such a challenge. I didn't see that side of her at all. We clicked. But her parents told me that the life lessons she gained around me made all the difference in Moriah's life. Maybe they were right.

While she was living with me, Moriah reconnected with an old flame, Iain, whom she had met in church. He had gone into the Navy, and they struck up a correspondence that turned into a romance. He planned to come to Denver to visit her, and wouldn't you know that the week he came was the week she finally got scheduled to do her clinical internship. They were so disappointed. They had planned to drive to Washington State so that he could ask her parents for her hand in marriage. But she had to be here all week, every day for her clinical.

After she got off on Friday, they hopped in the car and went ahead to Washington. Her parents agreed to the marriage, and they were officially engaged in the spring of 2014. Moriah asked me to be her matron of honor. I didn't realize that she held me in that high regard. I suggested she ask one of her friends, and she said plainly, "No, you must be there." It was a beautiful fairytale wedding.

He had secured a government job in South Dakota, and they moved there right after the wedding. I remember talking to Moriah about keeping house. She didn't keep her room very well while she was living with me. Let me be blunter. Her room was a disaster! I tried everything to convince her to do a better job. Finally, I suggested that a young woman engaged to be married should start taking better care of her room. After all, she would be marrying a navy guy, and part of his training included how to be neat and tidy. I asked her how he would feel if this is the way she kept house. She shaped up and cleaned up immediately!

It always amazes me how I have felt inspired and blessed by a person, only to learn that they were moved or encouraged by me. People often tell me that I inspire them. It's surprising to hear that when I've just met them. You never know. People are watching, and you never know when you might influence someone for good.

Key #53: Learn from the people around you and expect that they are learning from you.

M.U.S.I.C.
PART 4: I
IRREPRESSIBLE –
INDESTRUCTIBLE –
INVOLVED

Pursue your purpose **Irrepressibly**. When you are persistent and consistent in your pursuit, you will be **Indestructible**, regardless of what hardships come your way. Stay actively **Involved** in everything you do.

HAZEL RAMSBOTHAM

FOREWORD
BY PHYLLIS I. PIEFFER, NCTM

Hazel and I first met during my term as state president of the Colorado State Music Teachers Association 1981-1983, and have continued a long collegiality since then. I was very impressed with this new member of the Aurora Music Teachers Association who was such a dynamic force! She had more energy, enthusiasm, and endurance than most other teachers, and was so open to learning everything she could about teaching, about the organization, and becoming acquainted with all the members. And recently Hazel and I learned that we share the same birthday – April 1.

For Hazel, being a young girl growing up during the Depression years was not easy, especially in a family without a father. Her biography is a superb history of the American woman's movement from the 1930's into the 21st century. It is a book that will resonate with the #MeToo movement. It is a story of bravery and dignity in the face of authoritarian figures, prejudice against women, and discrimination toward women in the workplace. These are circumstances that many women piano teachers have experienced.

Through it all, Hazel held the strongest ethic to "Love God First." Second to that was to "Love Music." As a young child with perfect pitch, she would figure out melodies and accompaniments on her mother's piano before they could afford lessons. At age 6, she knew that she wanted to be a music teacher. Even then, lessons were sporadic as was college education in music. Despite numerous setbacks, she attained a Bachelor of Music degree in 1959 and a Master's degree in 1967. With those degrees in hand and membership in local, state and national music organizations, came opportunities to connect with master teachers and artists, such as Nelita True and Jean Barr at MTNA National Conferences and International Music Workshops. Hazel had a breadth of musical experiences that most teachers could not duplicate.

Hazel wrote that "Life is a musical composition that changes rhythm and direction at times but has the same themes woven together throughout the years and seasons." The chapters of her life story are organized by the letters in the word M U S I C.

M = Miracle, Magic, and Mastermind
U = Underwriter, Unafraid, Unshaken
S = Student, Searching, Spiritedly
I = Irrepressible, Indestructible, and Involved
C = Challenge, Conductor, Commitment

The lessons learned are expounded as (Piano) Keys 1 - 88. Key # 1 was her mother's voice saying to her: You really can do anything you want in life, as long as you want it badly enough." Hazel added, "Even when surprises try to convince you otherwise." And finally, Key #88, "Money is wonderful but it isn't the end prize." Her writing is creativity at its best – showing the perfect harmony of music to life.

This book is a testament to Hazel's commitment and dedication to music, to teaching, and to life. It should be read by every young person pursuing a music career and current and/or retired music teachers for the twentieth century social history it recounts. It will surely trigger many memories for older teachers and women.

I have the deepest admiration for what Hazel has accomplished in her lifetime. Most of us could not accomplish even half as much. And she accomplished her goals with a smile on her life, always believing that she could overcome the roadblocks. It challenges each of us to do more; to continue to play our instrument every day, to continue to connect with other human beings, sharing ideas and goals, and to not give up on anything as being too hard or impossible to reach.

Phyllis I. Pieffer, NCTM (Nationally Certified Teacher of Music). Pieffer holds a Bachelor of Music degree in piano performance from the College of Wooster in Wooster, Ohio, and a Master of Arts in music theory from Eastman School of Music in Rochester, New York. She has held numerous positions on local, state, and national levels of MTNA including President of Colorado State Music Teachers Association (1981-1983), President of the West Central Division of MTNA (1990-1992) and President of Music Teachers National Association (2003-2005). She has retired as an Independent Piano Studio Teacher, College Instructor, and Church Musician. Denver, Colorado

Our Family Band
Quentin, Ree, Roma, Roy, Ronda, Hazel, Randy

CHAPTER 11: INDESTRUCTIBLE: MENTAL AND EMOTIONAL FATIGUE

My relationship with my first husband, Quentin was a rollercoaster that left me mentally and emotionally drained by the time he deserted our family. He wanted to control everything the children and I did, and repeatedly accused me of infidelity whenever I did something on my own. Whatever my goals have been throughout my life, I believe everything was colored by what I experienced over the course of my first marriage.

Sometimes I'm asked how I got involved with Quentin in the first place. For your benefit, whether you are female or male, I think highlighting some details from my experience will help you in your relationship building.

When Quentin was young, he was very dashing, good looking and a lot of fun. He was as attracted to me as I was to him. I think music was the catalyst. Quentin was a very talented musician. He would sing and play the guitar, and I would play the accordion.

I was the first person Quentin had ever known that could play any song he wanted to hear. We played popular songs of the day and western songs. I could perform anything by ear, and he was amazed at that. He said I was the only person he had ever known that could play so well by ear. I taught all our children how to play the piano, and they all became outstanding musicians. My eldest son, Randy, played upright bass by the time he was only nine-years-old. He still performs professionally on the bass today. Roma, the oldest child, was playing concert caliber material by the time she was 11, and she became a piano instructor like I was. She has been teaching for over 50 years now.

Quentin was great at making up lyrics and poems. I remember one time we had a weekly live television show in 1953. The band leader and head singer had to be out for reserve duty, and Quentin was in charge of singing and leading the group. So, he was going to sing this obscure song. It wasn't very popular; few people knew it. Quentin could not remember the words to save his life. He kept messing it up.

So, when it came time for him to perform the song in the live television show, Quentin sang a line that wasn't in the song. I feared that he would mess up the whole song. But Quentin just sang another phrase that fit the song perfectly. And he did that through the entire song – messing up the lines and replacing the next one with something that fit. I was dying of laughter...on the inside! On the outside, I was trying to look like his improvisation was just how the song went and go along with it. He was so gifted.

Quentin was a lot of fun and had a humorous side that I enjoyed. I remember going to church one time when Roy was just a baby. Roy was always a little songbird, and even as a baby he would "sing" along with the congregation. One time when Roy was "singing" with exceptional gusto, Quentin leaned over to me and asked, in a soft voice, "Would you *please* step on his soft pedal?"

Quentin's relationship with our children varied considerably. Roma, Ronda, and Roy all had very mild personalities, and they rarely locked horns with their dad. But Randy and Ree's disposition was more volatile, and Quentin clashed with them. He picked on those two kids more than he did the others. It was very obvious to me and even to other people. Randy and

Ree could do no right, and the other three could do no wrong. I just could not understand that.

But Quentin enjoyed and wanted to teach our children how to be self-sufficient, especially outdoors in the wild. They learned a lot of survival skills from him, such as how to build a fire, how to clean and cook fish, and first-aid. He was very much of a teacher, and he loved to teach the kids when they were interested. For the most part, all of the children were interested in everything he shared.

Quentin wanted me to do everything he was interested in doing. He became a ham radio operator, and I had to get my ham license. I helped him study for his license, and I got mine at the same time. When he was in the Border Patrol, he had to learn Spanish, and I studied it right along with him. If he was working on the car, I was there, handing him tools. Quentin loved to hunt, so he got me a 300 Savage Rifle with a scope and taught me how to shoot, and I went with him. Eventually, all the children learned to hunt as well.

Once we moved to Lander, Wyoming, in the fall of 1959, hunting season became an essential part of the year for us because we ate the food. We hunted antelope and deer. Anyone who had a $5 license could get one antelope, and another $5 license would get them one deer per season. We butchered them, ground the meat, packaged and froze it. Meat from wild game fed us for most of the year.

I found it painful to shoot those beautiful animals, but we were not hunting just to hunt. We didn't waste a bit of the food. I loved antelope hunting because we could drive until we saw antelope, jump out and shoot. I learned to be a pretty good shot because once we got our quota, we were done for the day! Deer hunting was more strategic and involved sitting still and silent in the cold for long periods of time. That was never my style!

On one of our hunting trips, Quentin found a man lost in the woods and brought him back to our camper where we shared Thanksgiving dinner with him. The man was sure he was going to die out in the woods because he just could not find his way back to his camp. He was so grateful when Quentin rescued him.

Key #54: Even in unfortunate times, there are positive memories that are worth keeping with you forever.

However, all that companionship and camaraderie with Quentin began to change gradually. He couldn't make up his mind what he wanted to do with his life, and we spent a lot of time pulling our 15-foot camper trailer around the country headed toward one thing after another. We would travel to a new town for a job, or a college course, or something else. Whatever Quentin wanted to do, the children and I would follow along until the next idea entered his mind.

In the summer of 1969, Quentin decided he wanted to quit his teaching job in Lander, Wyoming and move to Taos, New Mexico to become an artist. I was not very supportive of this move. In fact, I was scared because he had tried other similar schemes that had failed. Like the time that Quentin wanted us to move to Delta and start a peach farm. By that time, he was getting increasingly bizarre, and I wasn't jumping on board anymore as I had at the beginning of our relationship. I did not start packing with excitement shouting, "Great! Let's do it!"

So, Quentin took his summer teaching pay (3 months) and went to Taos. He took all the money and left me at home with five children. I had to take care of everything while he was gone; the house payments, the utility bills, and our living expenses. I taught a limited amount of piano lessons in the summer to spend more time with the children, so it was hard for me to pay all the bills on my own.

The plan was for Quentin to help with finances at home once he started making money on his art, but he never did. And I did okay. In August, I went to a bank and asked the bank president (whose children were students of mine) if I could borrow $150 to make it through the summer. I explained where Quentin was and that I just needed a little extra. He was shocked. He couldn't understand why I would put up with it. But I explained I had no control over Quentin. He did what he wanted to do, and it didn't matter to him how it affected the children or me.

By August, Quentin was unable to pay his rent in Taos, so he decided he would come home. He called me on a Tuesday night, and I was much more gracious than I needed to be to him. Quentin told me he would be home Thursday. I said that was great, but I might not be home when he arrived because I had to take Randy to an event. But I assured him we would be back soon if we were not home when he got there. The other end of the line was silent. My husband had hung up.

Quentin did not come home Thursday. He didn't come home Friday. Finally, he came dragging home Saturday afternoon. He was angry at me and refused to speak to me because I had said I might not be home when he got there. And, as you might guess, he had no money for me. Life with Quentin declined from there. That was the summer of 1969. And he didn't leave until 1977. That is a long time to endure a relationship going downhill. Obviously, tensions were always high during those years, and it was a miserable way for a family to live.

One day, Quentin decided to make wine in the basement. I'm not sure what motivated him to begin this particular hobby, because no one in our family drank any liquor. But, by that time, he was beginning to do all kinds of things that didn't make sense. Quentin filled up some beer bottles with the wine he was making, but something went wrong. I don't know if it didn't ferment enough, or what, but all the bottles blew up.

There was glass all over the basement. Even after we cleaned it up, we were finding glass shards from the explosion for months later.

Quentin did all kinds of dangerous things. Today, he would probably be arrested for doing the things he did. But we didn't know. He just did whatever he wanted to do. One time, he decided he wanted to fly an airplane, so he took some flying lessons. And every time he flew anywhere, something seemed to go wrong.

Once, Quentin and I flew to see his mother in Wichita Falls, Texas, and on the way home, we had to crash land in Lamar, Colorado. I had been so trained to not say a word about anything that he did so that he wouldn't bark at me. There was a high wind as we were approaching the Lamar airport to land. I saw the ground coming up to meet us too quickly, but I didn't say a word. I just sat on my hands, and I didn't scream or say anything. We crash landed, and Quentin yelled at me to get out of the plane.

In the fall of 1974, Quentin moved us from town to property alongside the Yellowstone Highway outside of Lander, Wyoming. The property had an old, dilapidated barn with manure on the floors and cracks in the concrete. I agreed to the move because Quentin was getting the wander lust to go somewhere new and this allowed us to stay near Lander. The plan was to live in our camper and take the next year building our dream home up on the hill of the property. As part of our dream home, we planned to convert the barn into an art studio.

Well, the whole family worked as if we were slaves at that house every minute we could. We shoveled out the manure and installed sheetrock and ceilings. There was no running water, so we had to carry water in and use an outdoor toilet. We heated the barn with a wood coal stove.

I needed a place to teach, so we put my two pianos in the front of the barn where the stove was. To make it habitable for teaching, I would get up at 5:00 am to start the fire in the wood coal stove so that it would be warm enough to give lessons. That's when I would practice piano for an hour. By the time I finished, it was warm enough to wake up the children so that they could get ready for school. Then, I made breakfast for the family.

I had to cook using a little cookstove in the camper. I always made everything from scratch. It was challenging in those conditions, but my family ate biscuits and eggs with bacon every morning. Except for the mornings we had biscuits and oatmeal. My family loved biscuits! On occasion, I would make pancakes for a treat, but they always returned to their beloved biscuits.

We thought we would be living that way for just a year, but two and a half years later, we were in the same place. Amenities were so absent in that house that I didn't even have a place to take a shower. My husband was an art teacher in the high school at that time, so he and the children would shower at the school. But I had no place to wash. Quentin would let me into the school on Saturday nights after the sporting events were over and that is when I could take a shower—once per week!

For two and a half years, the children and I would spend all our spare time working on that house. Eventually, we finished one bathroom (although we had to haul water in to fill a cistern), and my studio, but we never were able to complete the rest.

Quentin started traveling on weekends as a manufacturer's representative for the Alpine Kiln Company. He told me we needed the extra money to finish the house. I couldn't argue with that; the place was a money pit! He would assign me and the children tasks to work on while he was gone, and that's what we would do all weekend. The kids rarely got to hang out with friends or do any normal activities other teenagers did.

Quentin insisted on having rock floors in the house. So, he would send me and my three youngest children, Ronda, Roy, and Ree on trips down to Colorado. He refused to pay for the rocks, so we had to go to a spot where we could pick them up and bring them home. We had to look for specific stones that were no thicker than one inch and flat. The kids and I would haul those rocks back for him to do the floor. It seemed like every time we went to that quarry, the truck would break down, leaving us stranded on the highway. Roy would run into town and find someone to help us get it going.

Those were rough times, mentally and physically. I remember a Fourth of July weekend; I was home with the kids working on the jobs Quentin had assigned while he left to attend a picnic on his own.

Roy asked: "Why is it that we always have to do everything, and he gets to do all the fun stuff? Let's just go to that picnic." So, we did. I was a little fearful to show up uninvited. But when we got there, everyone was thrilled to see us. They had wondered why we were not there earlier when Quentin arrived. They invited us too; Quentin just hadn't passed on the invitation.

Looking back now, I know we were in what today is labeled an "abusive relationship." At the time, I was emotionally drained, tired and overworked. I couldn't see the situation for what it was. But, I remember one incident clearly because, for me, it was finally the beginning of the end.

It was Valentine's Day of 1976. Ronda had to be at school at 6:00 am to catch a bus for a basketball tournament. It was freezing that day, about five below zero.

I woke up early in the morning and got ready to go. When I went out to warm up the car, I was unable to get any of our cars to start. Time was ticking, and I had to get Ronda to the school. So, I woke up Quentin. I apologized and explained that I did all the tricks he showed me to do but I couldn't get anything started.

He stormed out of the barn without a word, went to our Jeep and started it in no time at all. I just laughed and said it figures that would happen, in a happy kind of way. I thought Quentin would get out and let me into the jeep so that I could drive Ronda to school.

He growled, "Get out of the way!" I told him we needed to leave, and he barked again, "Get out of the way." That was when I realized he intended to drive Ronda, so I started back toward the barn. On the way, I pushed the door of the Jeep closed to get by. I didn't do it in anger; I wasn't even mad! But as I walked toward the barn, I heard shuffling behind me. As I turned around, Quentin grabbed my parka, spun me around and threw me down on the ground. He hit my head against the metal siding of the barn. Looking down at me, he shook his finger and snarled "Your temper! I'm sending you back to your Mother in Iowa Park!"

I don't know how I was able to remain calm, but I looked up at him coolly and said: "You have the nerve talking to me about my temper. Your daughter needs to get to the school, so get in that Jeep and take her." Poor Ronda was sitting in the car biting her nails wondering if she would get to school on time.

She made it. And when Quentin returned from taking her, I was waiting for him.

"Are you willing to talk about what just happened?" I asked.

"WHAT?"

"Do you want me to tell you what happened?" I then rehashed the events of that morning.

"Oh, how the story changes when you tell it," Quentin sneered.

"That's exactly what happened, and you know it. Now I just want to ask you one question. Do you think the way you acted is the way a man should treat his wife?"

"No," he conceded.

"Thank you," I replied. "I am taking that as an apology. But I will tell you one thing. Don't you ever lay a hand on me again. If you do, you are going to be behind bars. And I will take these children, and you will never see them again."

I guess he realized I meant it, so he never did try that again.

Key # 55: Stick up for yourself and your family when you need to.

Later that night, Ronda looked so relieved when I picked her up from school. She was afraid I had left the house and abandoned the family. No, I assured her I could never go off and leave her and the twins. But I did ask Ronda one thing: "What did I do that caused it to happen?" She replied: "Nothing mom. He is crazy."

So that's the way Ronda and the twins felt. They could see it evolving. I was glad that Randy and Roma were already out of the house on their own and didn't have to deal with Quentin's personality changes.

That Valentine's Day incident happened one year before

Quentin left. Turns out while he was away on weekends, he was doing more than selling kilns. We discovered Quentin had been fooling around with a 23-year-old music teacher who was also one of my piano students.

The three youngest kids still at home, Quentin, and I were still performing in our family band, and this woman would come to hear us play. She would stop out at the house as well. Fool that I was, I did not realize she was hanging around for a different reason. But then, she worked her way into a western band Quentin was part of in an old mining town called South Pass City. They would play in a bar there on Saturday night, and this gal started going up there and eventually worked her way into being a member of the band.

I finally caught on to what was going on, and by the following January, I had had enough.

Key #56: When enough is enough, that is enough!

On January 28, 1977, I disguised myself, borrowed a car, followed Quentin and his sweetie 150 miles, walked into their hotel room and shot them both.

With a camera.

But let me back-up and tell the whole story.

After I saw the motel they had stopped at, I went to the house of a friend that lived nearby. He didn't recognize me in my disguise, so I had to remove it. After I explained what was going on, he and his wife went with me to the motel.

My friend waited outside while I walked into the motel lobby and asked the clerk if there was a Quentin Roberts registered there. When he replied affirmatively, I said: "I'm his wife." The clerk looked like a cartoon character as the color drained right off his face until it was pale white. It was 1977. The wife of a cheating husband did not show up on the doorstep of their hotel room every day. His mouth dropped open, and he finally replied "I have always wondered if something like this was going to happen! What do you want me to do?"

"Just give me the key to the room."

"This is my motel. I don't want any trouble here. Do you expect trouble?"

"He won't have time to make trouble. He does carry a loaded 45 with him, but he won't have time to use it."

"Whoa!" exclaimed the motel owner. "Wait a minute and I'll call the police!"

"Go ahead. I already called the police and told them what I was going to do. They said they weren't going to do anything to protect me unless Quentin shot me. If he shoots me, the police will come. Thanks a lot!"

The man was pretty concerned. He told me he was calling the police anyway because he didn't want the place getting shot up. So, I went out to wait with my friends until they arrived.

I was nervous because I had taken off my disguise and I was afraid Quentin was going to come out of the room. The police finally arrived, and by that time, the motel owner and his wife, my friend, and his wife, I, the Chief of Police, and a deputy were all standing around outside of the motel room. It was quite a crowd.

The Police Chief noted that we only need a couple of people to go in. So, I went in with my friend, and we both started shooting pictures with our cameras. I pulled the covers off Quentin's sweetie and said, "Smile you are on candid camera!"

After the initial uproar, Quentin started yelling at me, demanding it was my fault. I calmly replied: "Tell it to the judge. Go ahead and blame. Everything has always been my fault the way you tell it."

I returned the key to the owner of the motel, and he looked at me with admiration. "Lady! You are the coolest thing I have ever seen in my life! I expected you to scream and yell and cry, but you are as cool as a cucumber."

"I shed all the tears over that man that I will ever shed again," I told him.

And I never did shed another tear over Quentin.

Key #57: Try not to cry over someone that hurts you. They don't deserve your tears.

I may have never shed a tear, but I had emotional scars nonetheless. We were married 27 ½ years, and we were very close to being empty nesters. That is when he chose to leave the family. I was devastated. I never wanted to be a career woman. I wanted to be a good mom, wife, and homemaker. Quentin's leaving knocked me for a loop. It was challenging financially, but even more so it was difficult emotionally. To feel Quentin's rejection after I had been so submissive, was overwhelming. Even though I knew the fault lay with Quentin, I could not help thinking over and over "What should have I done differently?"

Quentin and his sweetie married, and they ultimately had three boys. When their children were three, five, and seven years old, she left him and went back to Pennsylvania to live with her mother. Then he married again, and again, and again—five more times after me! I finally realized the break in our marriage must not have been my fault. It took a long time to come to that conclusion, though. Years.

That experience hardened me in many ways. Quentin never saw me cry. Our marriage did make me cry at times, but I would have never cried in front of him. And so, I got so toughened up that I would never weep about anything anymore. Today, it takes a lot to make me cry! I have to be emotionally touched to cry.

Key #58: Crying is not the only way to feel better.

Quentin died in 2005. There was no funeral. We heard that he had been diagnosed a couple of days before with cancer. He was already carrying around an oxygen tank by that time, so his general health must not have been very good either. He ended his life by shooting himself instead of going through the pain that accompanies cancer and its treatments. I didn't feel or care anything about it by that time.

I have suffered through a divorce and the death of my second husband, Buddy. Much as Buddy was the love of my life, and I was sad to lose him, I discovered it is so much worse to experience divorce than it is to suffer the death of a spouse. There are some reasons why I believe that.

First, when your husband dies, you cannot blame yourself. You do not feel rejection or believe in some way it is your fault. He hasn't left you on purpose, and you do not have the guilt because you have done everything you can do.

Second, if you have children and your marriage is healthy, there are usually no custody or visitation decisions to be made when one of the parents dies. Battling for these rights can be overwhelming.

Third, in a divorce, you not only lose your marriage but all your mutual friends as well. Everybody is afraid to take sides, so they ignore you. It can feel like you are invisible to people you used to talk with all the time. I had no one I could confide in who could come even close to understanding what I was going through.

When there is a death, it is final. You can go on with your life and start over. But with my divorce, Quentin was always around because we lived in a small town.

Divorce puts you in a horrible turmoil in your life. I thought my life was over and I was only 47 years-old. I have experienced a whole new life of 40 years since then! And it's been a lot more pleasant. But at the time I couldn't see there would ever be a positive outcome for me.

What are the lessons learned from this experience? Most important: People will treat you like you let them treat you. If you allow it, they will mistreat you. Remember, you are always in charge. Don't let anyone abuse you, mentally or physically.

Key #59: Know how you want to be treated and insist on it.

Roy, Ronda, Randy, Ree, Hazel, Roma, Shane

CHAPTER 12: IRREPRESSIBLE: STARTING OVER WHEN IT FEELS LIKE EVERYTHING, AND EVERYONE, IS OUT TO GET YOU

The divorce not only left me emotionally scarred but in financial jeopardy as well. I did not want my kids to have to leave the town where they were born and raised. It was the seventies, and I worried about them getting into drugs or other trouble if I yanked them up and took them to someplace new. I figured I would have to stay in Lander.

I'd known so many women who had been left widowed or divorced, and they jumped right into another relationship just for the financial security. To me, that was jumping from the frying pan into the fire. I would not do that. I would not put my kids or me through that kind of emotional roller coaster. I vowed that I would be there to be their mom and not worry about any personal life at all.

Honestly, the whole experience turned me into a man-hater for a while. My lawyer seemed to be on Quentin's side, not mine. I had married men coming on to me because I had the stigma of being a divorcee. I even had people coming by to "help" me with the house, and all they did was steal my tools.

Key #60: Beware of false help.

I had a terrible lawyer. First, he told me that I couldn't get alimony because I was too educated and could take care of myself. I couldn't believe it. I knew plenty of educated women who got plenty of alimony. I had borne the man six children and put him through college so that he could make a living for the family, and now my lawyer was telling me I didn't have a right to alimony.

My lawyer's response was that those women got alimony because their husbands did not fight about it. Quentin was going to battle. The result was that I received no alimony. I got $150 child support for the three youngest children at home. That's it.

We wound up splitting the property into two pieces. He would own the front part of the property and the camper trailer. I would retain ownership of the rear portion and the house. Looking back, I should have kept the property together to keep its value higher because that split ruined the value of my piece of the land and home. I was in a catch 22 because my lawyer told me that if I kept all the land, I would receive no money settlement from Quentin to finish the house. The house had a lot to complete, so I felt I had no choice but to split up the property between us.

I tried to get some advice from the husband of a woman I was friends with who was a successful businessman. But neither of them would even talk to me about it. They just said talk to your lawyer; we don't want to get involved. That's the way it was all over town. I had no one I could talk to, and my brothers and mother lived so far away. As it turned out, it was not a good arrangement, and the value of my property was damaged. It ended up that Quentin got more out of the divorce than I did.

Next, my lawyer told me he was going to bring Quentin to the house and let him take what he wanted to claim as his own. Here we were, living in still primitive conditions in an unfinished house, and apparently, he was entitled to any personal property he wanted. That made no sense to me at all, and that was certainly not the way the law should work, I felt. The only reasoning my lawyer would offer was, "Well, it will be easier this way."

I replied: "Not with the bloodshed that will happen if you bring him here. Listen, man, I have a 300 Savage Rifle with a scope, and I am an excellent shot! I also have an attack dog. Are you willing to take the chance?"

The final injustice came when I told my lawyer I wanted my divorce papers to state the divorce was on the grounds of adultery. He laughed and said "You can't get a divorce for adultery anymore! You can divorce for all kinds of things, but no one claims adultery anymore."

It was imperative to my family and me. My oldest daughter, Roma was living in California when all this happened, but I remember calling her for her birthday and telling her the sad news. Roma said to me: "Mom, that's not sad. Now you have a scriptural reason to leave him. I have been so worried he was going to kill you and bury you in the garden and no one would know where you were." The whole family knew the marriage was over, but the scriptural basis of adultery was fundamental. I would not change my mind on that matter. I told my lawyer that God allows divorce for one reason: adultery and so that's what it has to be. "Sometimes you might not get everything you want," he replied.

"I've never gotten anything I want," I replied firmly. "But I'm going to get this! This is the one thing I'm going to get."

The night before the divorce, he had all the papers ready for me to sign. "Does it state adultery as the grounds?" I asked.

"No."

"Then I'm not going to sign."

"But my secretary will have to type them all over again," as if that was the most critical issue.

"That's your problem," I insisted. "I was clear from the beginning that the divorce had to be on the grounds of adultery."

It was crazy how I couldn't even count on my attorney to look out for me. At first, I was incredulous. I could not believe it. But, unfortunately, that was not the last time people I thought were my friends and neighbors burned me.

Key #61: When hiring people for professional services, oversee their every move to assure you are getting the services you paid for.

After Quentin was gone a month, I went to the School District and applied for a job. I had all the teaching credentials I needed: both a bachelor's and a master's degree, five years teaching experience in a school and countless years teaching piano. But no, I was told I was over the hill (I was only 47 years old) and over-qualified. I hadn't taught in a school for 18 years and as far as they were concerned that made me incapable of teaching in the school.

Later, when I looked over the credentials of the 32 new teachers hired for the next school year, I could have qualified for at least 2/3 of the jobs because my education and experience was so varied. Eventually, I went to the principal who was a good family friend. I asked him why they didn't consider me for any of those 32 jobs.

"I didn't know you needed a job," he said.

"Jack! Don't try to kid me. You know what's going on. Everybody knows. How do you think I am going to make a living?"

"Hazel, we'd be tarred and feathered if we took you away from private teaching. Everybody in this town depends on you to teach their children piano."

"But Jack, I'd have to teach every evening and weekend day in addition to my current schedule to make enough money to raise my children. I am their only parent now. I don't want to be working at the only times I can be with my children. I need a job that matches their schedule."

"Don't worry," Jack soothed. "We'll find a place for you. Don't worry."

Well, wouldn't you know they never did find a place for me! When it was time for school to start, I went back and asked what they had.

"Well," Jack said, "there was an opening at the North School, but they decided it would be too confusing for the children if they had two Mrs. Roberts over there." Quentin's new sweetie worked at the North School.

I had another idea, so I went to the School Board again. Elementary kids who took a bus stayed before and after school for a while, and I suggested I offer piano lessons during their wait time. The parents would pay for the lessons, so all the School Board would have to provide would be a room with a piano. The band teacher and the choir teachers were all for it because it would feed musicians to their programs in Junior High and High School.

After I presented my proposal, the School Board turned me down. Their reason: If we allow you teach before and after school, we will have to let everyone do it.

"But nobody else wants to do it!" I exclaimed. This was such a small town; their reasoning seemed ludicrous to me. "Besides, no one else is qualified to do it."

"What do you mean?" they asked.

"If you had a seventh grader apply to teach physics in High School would you give them the job?"

"Noooo," they replied, "they wouldn't be qualified."

"Exactly my point," I told them.

So, they asked me my qualifications. I told them I am a nationally certified piano teacher. Nobody else in town had that certification.

Their reply to me was appalling. Remember this was a small town and I knew most of the people on the School Board and taught some of their children the piano. I thought they were my neighbors if not even my friends. But, they said to me, and I quote:

"Oh, I know what you're doing. You're just feathering your nest and wanting to cut everybody else's throat."

It was at that moment that I told myself I was getting out of Dodge. I was leaving that place. That was when I decided I was moving.

Key #62: When you have done everything you can, and things still are not in your favor, move on.

I was so upset with them for not giving me a job in the school. I concluded I had to move. You didn't commute up there in those winters. Our towns were too far apart, and the weather was terrible. I knew I didn't want to live in that house in those conditions having to haul water in the back of a truck to put in a cistern just to have running water. I didn't think that I wanted to do that when I was 70 years old. (That's what I considered old at that time: 70).

Roma, who was living in California at the time, had introduced me to a wonderful skin care line called Dynique It was made from the aloe vera plant, which was all the rage at the time. A multi-level marketing company produced and distributed the product. I didn't know a thing in the world about MLMs and certainly had no idea about skin care. But I loved the product, and when I saw the results, I decided to join the business as a representative for it. At that point, I was looking for any way to earn a buck.

I have no idea how it took off for me so quickly and easily. I have no secret of success. I just told people about it and had them try it. Women loved the product and bought it. I started making money. It was just so simple. It was effortless to do. I began to accumulate what's known in MLM businesses as a downline, where others I referred to the business signed up to promote the products too. Whenever they made sales, I got paid! And, they were having success too. It was a magical thing. I had never heard of anything like MLMs before, and I was attracted to the residual income. That was what interested me.

The Company started flying me out once a month to California for their conferences. In those days, I never traveled. It was something special to me. And they gave me the Omega watch I still wear today as a reward for my sales. I've never owned anything so luxurious in my life as that watch. I was, and still am, very proud of it.

Eventually, they asked if I would be willing to move to Denver to set up an office and be in charge of a region consisting of Wyoming, Utah, and Colorado.

That was very attractive to me, but I was trying to stay in Lander until the twins finished high school. A couple of things occurred, however, to spur the decision along.

First, Ronda became a representative for Dynique. She had just graduated from High School and was not interested in going to college. I think part of her decision was because she saw how I could not seem to get a job in my academic field despite two degrees. At any rate, Ronda was not interested in spending money for college, but rather in making money. She was excited about working with Dynique because it looked like it was going to give her a good future.

Secondly, my oldest son, Randy was in Trinidad, Colorado attending gunsmithing school on the GI Bill. He had married a young girl in 1974, and they had a 16-month-old son, Shane. While they were in Trinidad, she decided she didn't want to be married anymore. So, she just took off and left Randy with Shane.

Randy wanted to move to Denver when he finished school, and I knew he would need help with Shane. Randy, who had a charming personality and got along very well with people, started in with Dynique and was making money too.

And then, other things began to get me more interested in moving to Denver. Mother was campaigning for me to move back to Texas to be near her, but I didn't want to live in Texas. Denver was only a one-day drive to her, compared to two from Wyoming.

Ronda, Roy, and Ree begged me to stay in ski country. They all loved to cross-country ski, especially Roy who lettered in cross country skiing in high school. I knew Denver was a pleasant temperate climate—not too hot in the summer and not too cold in the winter. Compared to Wyoming where we were living, it seemed like the Banana Belt!

I decided Denver was the spot for me to enter my next phase

in life. I didn't intend to come in October. I was going to have Ronda and Randy help me get things started, and I was going to operate from Wyoming until the twins finished high school. Roy had recently knocked his mouth with his knees while jumping on a trampoline and lost four of his front teeth. While it didn't seem to bother him too much, it made me think twice about leaving. I thought that an occasional visit to Denver would be enough for the first eight months or so.

It wasn't long, however, until I realized that the twins in high school were getting along a lot better by themselves than Ronda and Randy were in Denver with the baby! I decided to move to Denver and visit the twins two times a month rather than the other way around.

I remember talking to Roy and telling him how sorry I felt for them because of everything that happened. I said I knew how embarrassing it was for them to be at the school where his Dad taught. I just felt so sorry for it. And Roy said: "Mom, we aren't worried about us, we are worried about you. You don't have to worry about us. We know right from wrong. You have enough trouble. We will never do anything but make you proud of us. So, don't worry about us." They were so on my side about everything.

Key #63: Be thankful and aware of the people who are on your side.

Then I did something I never thought I would do. As conservative as I've always been, I had never dreamed I would leave my twins up there alone in that partially finished house to finish school by themselves. If it were two boys or two girls, I would not have been able to do it. But Roy and Ree were a real team. She cooked for him, and he protected her and took care of the house. The church watched over them. The members of our church congregation were the only people who knew they were there living on their own without an adult in the home.

They did great their senior year. Roy lettered in three sports: cross-country track, field track, and cross-country skiing. Ree won the Stars of Tomorrow contest held by the Rotary Club with a piano piece she learned and practiced on her own, and she entered a beauty contest. Both were All-State in choir and band and had parts in the school musicals. They stayed very busy at school and managed fine without my being at their side to watch over them. I am so proud of how they handled the situation   together.

I would drive up to Lander every couple of weeks to get groceries and to visit. Often, little Shane, who was two-and-a-half would come with me. The drive could be quite treacherous in the winter when it stormed. We had a few trips that were downright scary! Sometimes, I wonder how we made it through that year. I was so glad once the twins graduated and I didn't have to make those trips!

Key #64: Trust your decisions.

Looking back at that first couple of years after the divorce, I realize now how I was evolving into the person I am today. For the first time, I made the decisions. I had to take care of my family and myself with no reliance on anyone else.

At that time, I was outraged. Yet, I had five children who were spurring me on, saying "Go get 'em, Mom. Go get 'em!" I am so blessed that my children were entirely on my side. I knew that I had to be strong for them and support them until they could be on their own. But they were so supportive of me; they were so supportive.

I had to get indignant. I had to get mean. I had to get to the place where I knew that no one could make me crazy. I determined that I would never again succumb to being a helpless woman.

I was going to be better than ever.

I was going to be rich.

I was never going to put up with that rubbish again.

That's how I got the urge and the edge to get to where I am today.

Key # 65: Get mad when it is time to get mad.

Ronda, Randy, Roma, Roy, Ree

CHAPTER 13: SLAPPED DOWN AGAIN/GOT UP AGAIN

When I first came to Denver, I chose not to teach piano right away. I was going to focus my entire attention on building the Dynique business. The prospects were exciting. Unfortunately, a little less than a year after my move to Denver, the company began to display problems.

When I started with Dynique back in Wyoming, it focused solely on skin care, and the product was fantastic. Then they added a cosmetics product line, but it became difficult for us representatives to make ends meet with the cosmetics. Everything came in cases of 6 or more per case. So, if a customer wanted to order a cherry red lipstick, I had to order six of that cherry red lipstick. The customer got their one, and I had five left that I had to sell to somebody else. And then somebody would want some other color, and I'd have to order 6 of those. It was the same thing with the eyeshadow, and the blush, and all the other cosmetics.

The representatives ended up having to hold a vast inventory of cosmetics so that they could supply their customers on the spot. I ended up building a stock worth about $15,000 wholesale.

Then, for an unexplained reason, the company went bust. I never got an official notice from them, but at the Summer Conference in 1980, I saw the handwriting on the wall. At the conference, they revealed that the skincare line would no longer be available, which was the foundation of the company.

Soon after that, the company simply folded.

Here I was, relocated to a new home, with no job and $15,000 of cosmetics inventory. What was I going to do? I hated to even think about it. But I needed to unload those cosmetics and get my money back.

Maybe you have heard of the ancient proverb: "Fall seven times, get up eight." Well, that's precisely what happened to me.

An acquaintance of mine from Dynique told me at that last company conference that she had had some success selling cosmetics in the various stripper clubs in Dallas. I thought about it long and hard. I had never even known anyone like a stripper in my entire life. But I decided that they are just humans, like the rest of us. So, I braced myself and went.

I talked to the manager of a gentleman's club on Colfax Avenue, one of the most known areas in Denver at the time for adult entertainment. He let us come in and provide beauty facials for his female employees. They went well, and he told me he owned three other clubs and that I was welcome to them as well. Eventually, I added several more clubs to my weekly itinerary.

I also started teaching piano students again in the afternoons, and then I would box up my cosmetics and start my rounds in the evenings. I would go to three or four clubs a night. It was quite easy. I just talked to the girls and made friends with them. They were very gracious and friendly to me.

I never saw so many naked bodies in my life, and so many shapes, sizes, and colors! I didn't realize that people came in so many different varieties! Back in the day when I was in school, we didn't disrobe in front of each other while getting ready for our gym classes. We were very well protected and very well shielded from changing clothes in front of anybody. So, I'd never had that kind of experience before where so many adult women were willing to unveil themselves to others. It was quite a revelation.

A few of the girls asked me one time: "Would you let your daughter do this?" I said I wouldn't. I had to be honest. It's just against what I have always taught them about being modest. I just couldn't do that.

I didn't tell them, but I thought that my daughters wouldn't do it. But, I didn't want to say that to them because I didn't want to embarrass them or put them down.

Key # 66: People are just people.

Selling cosmetics, and later jewelry, to the stripper market made me realize that people are just people. They are the same everywhere. Everybody wants to better themselves. Most of these girls did not see it as a profession. They were there because they were in school or looking for another job, and it was good money for the number of hours worked. I hadn't thought of that until I talked to some of them. It wasn't something that they grew up thinking that when they grew up, they were going to be strippers.

That experience brought home the understanding that God made us all. And God isn't prejudiced. He makes us all, and he makes us all different. That's a fantastic thing to me. We all have mouths, and eyes, and hair and ears and noses, but there are no two people alike. Everyone is different.

Key #67: God isn't prejudiced. Why should we be?

Accepting people of all types and backgrounds has helped me grow in the Juice Plus business too. I learned that we have to accept people where they are and work with people where they are. We can't make someone do what we want them to do or stop them from doing what we do not agree with. What we can do is be a good example ourselves for others to see. Then, if requested to help, we can offer guidance to help them succeed.

Everyone has to be able to interact with people. Juice Plus is so different from having an office job. If you are out there doing something that involves a product, you have to be able and willing to work with people on every level. I think it is fascinating. It is certainly never dull trying to help people better themselves.

The key to working with people, in any job, is to find their need and fill it. You do this by asking a lot of questions. Get curious about people. Find out what they are doing, and if they like what they are doing. Ask what their dreams and goals are, and their plans to achieve them, if they even have any plans.

You just find out about people. It's just like making friends. People don't always care about other people; but, they always care about themselves. You have to find out what they feel and like. Listen more than you speak. That has not been an easy thing for me.

Key # 68: Find people's needs and fulfill them.

I worked with strippers for seven or eight years. I added costume jewelry to my product line because it went along well with my cosmetics, and I could make a little extra money. I was struggling to try to make enough to keep my house here in Denver. It was difficult to sell the property in Wyoming because the US Steel Mill had gone out of business and took 400 families with it. After high school, Roy got a job up there and was eventually able to sell the Wyoming property on a lease/purchase option. That is how, by the grace of God, I was able to buy the house I live in now.

The plan was for me to share the payments for this house with Ronda and Randy, who were living with me. But they soon married their honeys and moved out. I still had to keep up the house payments. That was another tough part of my life.

I still had cosmetics to recoup, and I added the costume jewelry line because it went well with the makeup. The girls just loved those belly chains and ankle bracelets. I kept depleting the cosmetics and at the same time making a little extra money with the jewelry. Those were lean days, very lean days.

Key #69: Even in times of diversity, expect at least some things to fall into place. Be grateful when those times happen.

Harold, Hazel, Mother, James

CHAPTER 14: LOSS

While not everyone has to deal with difficult financial times or the mental and emotional damage that comes from a painful divorce, it is highly likely you will experience the loss of a loved one at some time in your life. The grieving that comes with loss can be devastating. I am no stranger to grief. I already shared the heartbreaking experience of losing my first child at birth and Buddy's death, but those were not the only losses I have suffered.

We lost my brother, Charles, in Vietnam in March of 1967. Charles was my closest sibling, only fifteen months older than I was. Charles was very inventive as a boy. He loved to tear things apart and put them together. My mother didn't know what to do with him. I remember when Mother sat him in the front row in church so that he would behave. He took a watch entirely apart and put it back together during the sermon.

Charles had a 13-year-old Dodge '33 car when he was in high school. People in those days would trade their cars in every 2 or 3 years, so we thought that was the oldest car ever. These days my Toyota is 21 years old, and I don't even think about it. But Charles fixed up that car in all kinds of ways. He gave it an automatic start and a glove compartment light. It even had electric windows. Those were unheard of in cars in those days! He was terrific at all the creative things that he did.

After High School, Charles became a test pilot. He was the first person to bail out from an ejector seat and live to tell about it. He was written up in the 1951 Aviator Yearbook for that accomplishment. Charles had been on a regular maneuver in California, and his plane failed. He knew he had to bail out and as soon as he hit the ejector and cleared the plane, it blew up in smoke. During his descent, his parachute failed to open. It finally did open only a few feet off the ground and just in time for him to plow into a plateau in the San Bernardino Mountains. Two guys in a jeep saw him crash, so they drove up there and took him to safety.

Mother was visiting my Uncle Eddie Dean in California that week. Uncle Eddie was a Western musician and movie star in the 1940s. Charles went over to Eddie's place that evening and asked his Mother if she had heard about the cadet that crashed in the San Bernardino Mountains. "Well, it was me," he said when she said she hadn't.

My aunt thought Charles was teasing Mother. She took Mother into the kitchen and said "Does he tell tales like that all the time? He should not do that! Scaring you like that is a terrible thing to do to a person! You shouldn't let him do that."

When they walked back into the living room, the story about the crash was on the news. It told all about it and even mentioned Charles' name. It just proved his point, and he didn't have to say anything.

Key # 70: People might doubt what you say but have to believe what you do.

Eventually, Charles moved up through the ranks to colonel. He served in the Korean War and flew two One Hundred Missions in Korea. To get promoted to the next level, Charles had to make another overseas tour. He was 39 years old when he volunteered to go to Vietnam. Charles left on March 1 of 1967 and March 4 he was being flown around in an F4 plane to orient him to the area. That is a two-seater where the pilot sits in front and the passenger right behind him. Charles was in the back seat and had no controls. We never heard from Charles again.

He was in Vietnam for four days. And we didn't know for a long time whether he was captured or died. It finally was determined that the pilot flew into a mountain. I'm sure that if Charles were manning the controls, the crash would not have happened. As it is, they were both killed.

We didn't know for years if Charles was a prisoner of war or not. It was a strange situation. My middle brother James was a teletype operator in the military in Hawaii. The news came over the teletype that Charles was missing. Immediately, he called my brother in San Antonio and told him to go to Mother's and tell her in person. So, Mother got the news from her son before the Air Force got there. My brother James got in trouble for doing that because it was against military protocol. He just told them, "If you think I'm going to sit there and see my brother's name as MIA come over the teletype and not tell my family, you are wrong. I'm sorry. But I couldn't do that. I just can't obey those rules."

Key #71: Sometimes breaking the rules is the right thing to do.

I was living in Lander, Wyoming when the news of Charles' disappearance arrived. When I called Mother, who was in Iowa Park, Texas, I asked her what we should do. She said, "There is nothing we can do because he is just missing. We don't know if he is still alive or not. So, we have nothing to do. There is no point in you coming down here. I am fine and trying to deal with the news the best way I can."

The uncertainty of a family member gone missing is a horrible feeling because you do not know the details of what happened. It was 12 years before they changed Charles' status from missing in action to killed in action, and 23 years before we received his remains back and were able to have a memorial service for him at Arlington National Cemetery. The service was exceptional and mirrored the ceremony they had for President Kennedy: the military parade, horse-drawn carriage, the 21-gun salute, and even the fly-by.

Everyone grieves differently, so it is hard to give advice how to go through such a situation. At first, I was angry. It seemed so senseless. Then I was proud because Charles was doing his duty. And there was no one to blame. He knew that he was in danger when he signed up for the tour of duty. Of course, I was so sad to lose a close member of the family. But everyone has to grieve in their way.

Key #72: Honor your grief.

I always felt that life is for the living. We have to have our grieving time, but then we have to carry on. There is no point in living in the past. God knows your heart. I think we need to learn to carry on and continue despite adversities. The Bible teaches that we grow stronger from hardships and misfortunes, and that is how we build character. If nothing ever went wrong, we would probably turn into a bunch of wimps. We would fall apart when any little thing did not happen as we expected.

Key #73: Life is for the living.

I had calamities in my life from the time I was five years old. I guess that has carried me through all the other challenges in my life. But nothing prepared me for the anguish and regret that I experienced with the death of my granddaughter, Jara.

I don't like to talk about what happened to Ronda's daughter, Jara. But, this book and my 88 keys would not be complete without including some details of this event. She would be 29 years old now. She died in an automobile accident in 1997, and I was driving the car.

Ronda had two children, Joash, who was 11 and Jara, who was 9. They lived in Southern California, and the kids would visit me for a couple of weeks in Denver over the summers. In the summer of 1997, Joash and Jara attended the Wyoming Bible Camp, and then came to Denver to visit with me. I was to drive them back home to California in July. I was careful to stop every two hours and get out of the car and walk around to stay alert.

To this day, I do not know what happened to cause the crash. I don't think I went to sleep, but I must have blacked out for some odd reason. The car veered off the road, and when I opened my eyes I overcorrected, and the car rolled. It was totaled. Joash and I were in the front seat and strapped into our seatbelts. But Jara had undone her belt when she laid down to sleep in the back seat. I did not know that she took her seatbelt off, and when the car rolled, she was thrown from the automobile. They declared her dead on arrival at the hospital.

Of all the things that have happened in my life, that was the most horrible event of them all. I just kept asking God why he didn't take me instead of Jara. Why did I live? I was at the end of my life. My kids had grown, and I didn't have any responsibilities. But this child's life was just beginning when it was snuffed out. It was horrible. I had nightmares for a year. I thought that her mother and dad would never speak to me again. And I don't know how it happened. It haunted me for years.

I could not bring myself to drive a car for more than a year. My car was totaled, and I did not see any point in getting a replacement. Buddy drove me because I just would not do it. It took me a while. And even when I did start driving again, I refused to take anyone with me as a passenger for two full years. Now, I will take people in my car on occasion, but am adamant about seatbelts. I won't move the car until all passengers securely fasten their belts.

The whole situation surrounding the accident was horrible. But, when I returned home after the funeral, I started right back into teaching piano. Ronda was selling Tupperware at the time, and she went right back into her Tupperware business.

We were both criticized by family and friends because we went back to work so quickly. But, I think that's the best way to get over something; to get busy with your life. It doesn't accomplish anything just to sit around and cry and grieve all the time. That's not my style of doing things. I had a lot of tragedies and misfortunes that I've had to face, but I've just gone on with what I need to do, rather than stay in the state of stupor.

Key #74: When you need to get over something, get busy with your life.

CHAPTER 15: PERSEVERANCE

If there is one thing that adversity teaches, it is perseverance. As you might have guessed, at this point in the book, my first lesson in perseverance came from Mother. Mother believed that a good education led to a successful life, and, although she was a teacher, she did not help my brothers or me with our homework. Many parents today spend large amounts of their free time helping their children with their homework. This is a foreign concept to me!

My mother never helped me with my homework. If I asked a question, she would always tell me to try it myself, and then try again. Try on my own three times. If I couldn't do it after that, then she would see if she could help me. But she rarely had to, because, by the time I'd tried it three times, I could do it.

Key #75: Try three times before asking for help.

I think that perseverance develops self-esteem. These days, you always hear about people wanting to "teach" self-esteem, but you can't teach it! Self-esteem doesn't come from a book, or from a lot of empty compliments, but from doing something worthwhile, overcoming obstacles and succeeding.

During my years teaching piano, I always had a traveling trophy for each of my group classes. Every month each student in the group would perform for the other students and me. There were specific rules the students had to follow. For example, they had to bring their music on performance day, and if they didn't bring it, they were disqualified. If they stopped a piece and started again, they were disqualified. If they said anything during their performance, they were disqualified. There was a certain way they were to approach the piano and begin, and a certain way they were to conclude their piece and return to their seat.

The other students and I judged them on all the criteria, and if they didn't do it correctly, they were not eligible to win the trophy. The students were conscientious to ensure that their friends did what they were supposed to do, and they took the job very seriously.

That didn't mean they had to play perfectly. The students could make mistakes, but they had to go on. If they made an error but went on with the piece, they could still win the trophy. Hardly anyone played perfectly, but they had to play professionally, which meant that they should ignore their mistake, and go on.

I tried to teach my students that playing the piano was emotional as well as technical. I would tell them music is like a river. It flows. But once the river comes to a bend or a boulder or a rock, it doesn't stop. It keeps going around or over it. The same goes for music, and, for that matter, for life. The second you stop playing, it quits being music.

Key #76: The second you stop playing, it quits being music. So, don't ever stop playing.

So, each month, we would all vote on who did the best job, and that student would get to take the trophy home for the following month. At the end of the year, the one student that won the trophy the most times during the year would get to keep it. The kids would work like crazy to get that trophy. It was a very motivational push for them to work hard.

What I wanted my students to learn is that when something

disappointing happens, such as being disqualified for the trophy that month, the experience helps them to grow up.

When you get out into the world, the world is harsh. The world is not going to coddle you. That's why they needed to learn to face setbacks and figure out how to keep their disappointment from happening again. When students studied from me, they learned more than just piano. They learned more than music. They learned life lessons. So many of my students have come back and thanked me for that.

Key #77: The world is not going to coddle you. Learn from your setbacks.

I have a plaque on my studio wall that has always been my sentiment as to why I taught piano. It reads:

Why I teach Piano:
Not because I expect you to major in music.
Not because I expect you to play or sing all your life.
Not so you can relax and have fun.

But:

so you will be human
so you will recognize beauty
so you will be sensitive
so you will be closer to the infinite beyond this world
so you will have something to cling to
so you will have more love, more compassion, more
gentleness, more good...in short, more life.
Of what value will it be to make a prosperous living
unless you know how to live?

I ran a very tight ship, and because of it I had families that drove long distances to have their children study with me, and other families who sent all seven or eight of their children to me over the 35-year span I taught in Denver. Not every parent agreed with my strategy, however. I remember one family who sent their two children to train with me. The first month, the children told their parents about the trophy custom. Both parents were public school teachers, and they didn't like the idea of any competition. They approached me and suggested that the practice was discriminatory. And another parent indicated that some of my rules related to the trophy competition were unfair.

My response to any parent who questioned my teaching practices was to remind them that I ran a private studio and that if they disagreed with my curriculum, they were free to transfer to another teacher. I believed then and still believe now, that my program rewarded those students that worked hard and did well. I never put the other students down, and they had as even a chance to win the trophy as anyone else.

I also encouraged the parents of my students to give their children the opportunity to major in music if they desired by committing to musical instruction for the long term. Music is the only vocation that you can't wait to get to college to decide you want to pursue.

To be accepted in college for a musical degree, you have to have the background before you get there. That is the primary reason why I insisted that all my children learn to play piano fluently. Not because I expected them to have a career in music, but because I felt so inadequate all those years and had to work so much harder than others because I hadn't had that early training.

When a child is six years old, they have no idea what is going to happen in the future. If they decide when they grow up that they want to be a musician, it's probably too late. If a parent gives them the gift of music training to start with, then the child can decide later what he or she wants to do with it.

The importance of early musical training became real to me when I attended Ree's high school graduation ceremony. Both Ree and Ronda were members of the girl's swim team in high school even though neither had done much swimming before that. Not having any involvement in an organized school sport until high school and then trying to join a team, is quite a challenge! They both worked their way up on the team to become captain during their respective senior year (Ronda was a year ahead of Ree in high school).

After the ceremony, the girl's swim coach sought me out and told me that he had never seen girls work so hard and improve from where they started to accomplish what they did. He said he couldn't figure out what drove them to do it. Then, he told me, "I realized that it was because of their music training. They learned how to set goals and developed perseverance because of their music training." I am so glad he told me he had recognized the connection between music and mental determination. Most parents do not connect the dots between music training for their children and how all those hours of practice and tediousness pay off in other areas as they grow up.

Key #78: Introduce children to music very early in life.

Of course, there are many ways to enjoy music without making a career out of it. Accompanying singers at church or in school is a great way to go. But if a person wants to teach piano, I believe they should have a degree in music and training to teach piano. Anybody can hang out a shingle that says, "Piano Lessons." They don't have to know a thing. You have to have a license to do someone's nails or cut their hair, but you don't have to have a license to teach piano.

Your clients will probably not know whether you know anything or not. I think it is a shame because you can ruin a person's talent if you teach them wrongly. That's why I believe that the National Music Teacher's Association started a certification program, to identify those instructors with the musical credentials needed to teach. I became nationally certified the first year it was offered, and I have been a nationally certified piano instructor for 50 years as of 2017.

I attended National Music Teacher's Association conferences regularly throughout my teaching career. At one meeting I learned about the International Music Workshop at a reception they held to build awareness. Nelita True was a well-known international concert pianist whom I had met at previous conferences, and we were friends. She encouraged me to attend the International Music Workshop in Graz Austria that year. I had just received my flying privileges thanks to Roy's becoming a commercial pilot and decided I could afford the trip.

After I attended that first workshop, it was so fabulous that I vowed I was never going to miss another one. I traveled to some exotic locations including Brisbane Australia, Stavanger, Norway, Biarritz, France, and Graz, Austria. I prepared a scrapbook of many of my trips when I attended the workshops, and I enjoy reliving those fabulous trips when I look back at the pictures and stories in those scrapbooks.

Not only did I receive excellent musical instruction on a variety of topics while attending the workshops, but I had the opportunity to present a short seminar on any topic I wanted. Attendees and instructors alike would attend the workshops. There were some very prestigious instructors throughout the years, many from the Eastman School of music, including Tony Caramia and Jean Barr. We had classes all day, every day and three concerts each day. The workshops lasted four days, and then we had a day off for an excursion and then another four days of classes and concerts. The event was so fulfilling.

At first, I was worried about presenting a workshop to all those great musicians who seemed to know everything about music already. I told my friend, Nelita, who had convinced me to attend, and she assured me that she learned something new every time I gave a workshop. She told me that I should never take a backseat to anyone and to teach things I knew. Never assume that just because I knew something that everyone knew it.

That advice encouraged me a lot, so I just taught them what was on my heart and mind at the time. One time I showed them the rules on how to notate a composition. Another time I did a workshop on how to teach a student how to play by ear.

I learned at the International Music Workshops that nobody knows everything! There is always something more you can learn. I encourage you to attend workshops and seminars in whatever your chosen field, because not only will you come home with more knowledge, but you will come back inspired to achieve more. I would always come home from those conferences wanting to learn more music; wanting to practice more and to get better. Consider a plant. It is never going to stay stagnant. It is going to grow, or it's going to rot. The same goes for people.

Key #79: When you lose your desire to improve, you may as well be dead.

I can't reflect on the topic of perseverance without sharing my experiences with Jason Geary. Jason was a student of mine, who didn't start playing piano until he was thirteen years old. Jason's family moved to Denver from California when he was 14 years old. One of the mothers of a student of mine told me I should meet Jason and give him lessons. She kept saying he was fabulous, but, of course, she didn't know much about music. Finally, Jason and I met in the fall of 1990. ·

Jason had received one year of piano lessons from another instructor by the time he came to my studio for an interview. He walked in empty-handed, and we sat down in my studio at the Grand Piano. I asked Jason what he had been playing. He told me he was accompanying the choir at Overland High School in Aurora, Colorado. I couldn't believe it. It is not easy to accompany a choir even after many years of lessons, so to do it after one year was impressive.

I asked Jason to play something for me. He said he was playing Rhapsody in Blue, but the library made him bring the music back. I said that was okay because I had a copy he could use. His statement floored me, but I didn't let on. Rhapsody in Blue is a piano solo with an orchestral accompaniment. It is 30 pages long and a very challenging piece. Jason played some of the composition for me and did very well. I was amazed.

I asked: "What do you want to do with your music?"

Jason replied: "I would like to become a concert pianist, but do you think I've waited too long? I'm already fourteen, and I haven't had any real training. A lady down the street taught me a little bit before we moved and that is all."

"True," I replied, "most concert pianists start much earlier, but it looks like you have made up for a lot of lost time already. Can you play scales?"

Jason ripped out a scale for me.

"Do you know all of the scales?" I asked. He replied yes. "How did you learn them?"

"I bought a scale book and learned the fingering on my own," he replied.

I was fascinated. "You need to practice your scales with a

metronome," I suggested.

"I have one," he replied eagerly. Most kids don't want to practice with a metronome, and you have to beat them over the head to do it. But he had bought one with his own money.

I was getting increasingly intrigued by this kid. But I was cautious. Usually, a person who plays as well as he did doesn't think they need instruction.

Finally, I asked: "Are you willing to listen to what I say and to take my instruction? Because if I start teaching you, we will not always agree, I can assure you. But you are going to have to realize that I'll be the teacher and you'll be the student. And if you're not willing to go by that, then I can't teach you."

Jason just looked up at me standing next to him at the piano and said: "I'll do whatever it takes."

So, he came and started studying with me. And he worked very hard. Jason had tons of natural ability, but he was motivated as well. The first year we worked together, he won the State Steinway competition and got to play in Keystone with the National Repertory Orchestra. Jason just blew everybody away. It seemed like every contest he entered he won.

His talent didn't go to his head, however, which is an excellent trait for a young person to have. When I first started teaching Jason, I had two students that were working on their senior recital, and Jason was in the same group lessons as they were. They arrived one day before Jason did, and one of them asked me: "Miss Hazel, how do you account for Jason? We have worked our butts off all these years, and he comes in and plays circles around us!"

The other student chimed in, "Yeah, and he is so nice. We can't even hate him for it!"

I laughed and replied, "Honey, there is no accounting for Jason. He has a God-given talent, and there is just no accounting for him."

Jason and I did lock swords, a few times. He wanted to inhale everything as quickly as he could, and I preferred having him focus on one piece at a time until he mastered it. When Jason arrived at his first lesson, he had a stack of ten Concertos that he had borrowed from the library. I asked, "What would you like to work on?" He answered that he wanted to learn a Concerto and so he would play these ten. I told him we needed to settle on one, but he couldn't understand why. That's how he was.

Jason's parents would ask him to stop playing sometimes and give them some peace. I let him come over to my place and practice. One Saturday he came over and brought a sack lunch, and he practiced all day long. He had dedication. That was for sure. Around five in the afternoon, he came out to the yard where I was gardening to say goodbye to me. He asked if I remembered the Schumann Concerto he wanted to learn. I replied in disbelief, "You did not go out and buy that music, did you?" He was always spending his money on music. But Jason said no, he found it in my music cabinet and had played it during his lunch break. A concerto is pages and pages! And he played it during his lunch break for fun!

After he graduated, Jason attended San Francisco Conservatory. The first year there he entered a contest and won $2,500 and an all-expense paid trip to New York City to play in the Alice Tully Hall at Lincoln Center.

During his Junior year at the Conservatory, Jason won the Conservatory Concerto Competition. That time I bought my ticket to see him play with the San Francisco Orchestra. His mom came with me. It was amazing to see him working with the orchestra. He performed a Brahms Concerto.

His orchestra teacher told me that if I ever got more students like him to send them his way. He told me that if Jason got lost during rehearsal, he could improvise in the style of Brahms. He was awesome.

Jason was so well-liked that when he won the contest, the whole student body stood up and cheered because not only was he great, but everybody loved him. I replied to his orchestra teacher that I doubted I would ever have anyone like Jason again.

Jason went from the San Francisco Conservatory to Ann Arbor Michigan where he got his master's degree, and on to Yale. While he was working on his Doctorate there, he received a Fulbright Scholarship in Berlin Germany. Today, Jason is the Head of the School of Music at the University of Maryland in College Park. He was dogged in the pursuit of his goals, and even though he had the innate talent he needed to meet them, he spent hours and hours working to develop his skills as well. Jason is an ideal example of how hard work and talent can work together to reach monumental levels of success.

Key #80: Talent isn't enough. You need hard work to reap success.

It was an honor to train Jason and help him reach his goals. When I think of where he has gone, I realize that I had a part in not only inspiring Jason to succeed but also so many other people on whom he had an impact. It is awe inspiring, and I am proud to know I had a part in it.

HAZEL RAMSBOTHAM

M.U.S.I.C.
PART 5: C
CHALLENGE – CONDUCTOR – COMMITMENT

Always have a **Challenge** to strive for. Without goals, you will never achieve your life's purpose. You are the **Conductor** of your life, and you have to stay focused and **Committed** to the end prize.

HAZEL RAMSBOTHAM

FOREWORD
BY JASON GEARY, PH.D.

It was not until some 10 years after I first met Hazel Roberts-Ramsbotham that I realized she had a truly extraordinary life story to tell. It was the early 2000s and I was spending the year in Berlin on a Fulbright grant to complete dissertation research for my Ph.D. in music at Yale University. Hazel was in Europe—again—attending an international piano teaching conference, and my wife, Helen, and I had arranged to meet up with her in Berlin. After we had finally said our goodbyes, Helen and I turned to each other in disbelief at how much energy and zest for life my former piano teacher possessed at her relatively old age—and how many colorful and captivating stories she had to tell about the road that had led to the amazing life she was living. Now, almost 20 years later, it's clear that, at age 88, Hazel hasn't slowed down one bit, proof of which is the inspirational book you are currently reading.

When I first met Hazel in 1990, I was 15 years old and desperate to find the right piano teacher after having moved to Denver from California. I found in Hazel someone who was passionate about both music and teaching and who I felt had the necessary patience and expertise to guide a budding young pianist who was equally passionate about music but who was largely self-taught and who was in need of much refinement at the keyboard. During my time as her student, I caught glimpses of her life outside of music, but I was much too focused on my future career path—and probably too young besides—to really appreciate the unique aspects of her approach to life.

I certainly knew her to be a highly principled woman of deep faith and conviction, and I could see firsthand how important family was to her, especially the close bond she had with her children and grandchildren. I was also the beneficiary of her kind and giving spirit, which included free extra lessons ahead of competitions, opening up her house to me on weekends so I could practice on a grand piano, and driving me all the way from Denver to Salt Lake City so I could participate in the Gina Bachauer International Young Artists Competition. It was during this long road trip that I gained some insight into the incredible variety of formative experiences that had shaped Hazel's values and beliefs, but, again, it wasn't until I was somewhat older that I came to understand just how unusual it was to encounter someone who had the ability to channel these often painful and harrowing experiences into such a positive and upbeat outlook on life.

In the pages of this book, Hazel shares in intimate detail many of these same stories that I heard as a teenager and later as a doctoral student in Germany. With her characteristic warmth and humor, she offers an autobiographical account of her life from her childhood days picking cotton beneath the blazing Texas sun to her second career as a top salesperson for a dietary and nutritional company following her retirement from teaching piano after 74 years! Along the way Hazel shares the many lessons she has learned—cleverly presented as her 88 keys to health and happiness, one for each key on the piano— and offers her unique perspective on aspects of life including love, marriage, career, money, health, and family. As she tells the story of her long and rocky first marriage, readers will be drawn into the sheer drama of events that could be taken straight from a Hollywood script, but at the same time will be moved by the depth of emotion, vulnerability, and human frailty while gaining inspiration from Hazel's resilience and her resolve to forge ahead in search of a brighter future.

Woven together by a narrative thread that is at turns joyful, comedic, painful, pragmatic, and motivational, Hazel's story is ultimately one about the triumph of the human spirit amid life's trials and tribulations. In Hazel's case, this triumph rests on the foundation of an abiding faith and an unyielding love of music. And like that love of music, Hazel's optimism, energy, and positivity is infectious. These qualities shine through on each and every page of this book. I am confident that, with Hazel's help, you too can unlock the keys to living a long and happy life.

Jason Geary, Ph.D.
Professor and Director, University of Maryland School of Music
April 10, 2018, Bethesda, MD.

Back Row: Allen & Ree, Roma, Ronda & Jonathan
Front Row: Roy, Hazel holding Joash, Mother, Shane, Jan
holding Lynnsey, Randy

CHAPTER 16: GETTING AN EDUCATION – NO MATTER HOW LONG IT TAKES

Goals make life worth living. If we don't have something to strive for, we are just marking time from day to day. There have been a lot of valuable goals in my life, but probably the most significant for me was the desire to get my education no matter how long it took.

I never even thought about going to college when I was growing up; we didn't talk about it. Mother was a teacher, however, and always said that she wanted us to get an education. Our daddy didn't have one; he had only been through the fourth grade. Because he was the oldest in the family, he had to quit school and go to work.

In my teens, I worked at the Norsworthy Music Center in Wichita Falls, teaching accordion from age 15 until I was 19. I would take the Continental Trailways bus every Saturday morning at 7:00 am and walk eight city blocks to the music store with my accordion in tow. It weighed around 35 pounds, and I would have to stop and rest one or two times before I could go on. My senior year of high school the store would send a Cadillac for me every day after school. I didn't think anything of it at the time but later in life, I attended a school reunion, and one of my friends told me they were so envious of that car. They all thought I was something. I had no idea.

There wasn't another Trailways Bus until 6:00 pm, so the store provided me with a practice room in the afternoon. They let me use any of the music on the shelves while I was there, so I would pick up the sheet music for the latest songs of the day, practice them until I had memorized them, and return the music to the shelves at the end of the day. I didn't have any money so that I couldn't buy anything, so I would spend the entire day on Saturday practicing.

I finally had money, but I didn't want to spend a single penny of it. I was saving it all to attend college. I already described how I attended Harden College, which was a two-year school at the time. I was putting in a lot of hours assisting the Head of the Music Department, working at the Norsworthy Music Center, and taking 21 class hours.

After I completed my two years at Harden, I wanted to attend North Texas Teacher's College in Denton, Texas, which later became University of North Texas, one of the famed music schools in the country. But my mother discouraged it. I wound up marrying Quentin and did not go to school again for seven years.

Quentin was working for the federal government with the Border Patrol in 1952-1954. I was so proud of him because it was such a difficult job to get. We went to Las Vegas to visit his older brother. Quentin loved the hot, dry climate so much that he decided he wanted to move there.

He returned home to Texas and asked for a transfer to Las Vegas. It was a long shot since there are no borders in Las Vegas, but he was still angry when the government denied his request. He walked off the job and resigned, and we moved to Las Vegas, with no position or other prospects lined up. I was eight months pregnant with my second child, Randy, at the time.

We went to Las Vegas, and Quentin went to work as a welder in his brother's welding business. He was working with cumbersome equipment and started having heart attacks. His health deteriorated to the point where he couldn't even go up and down stairs, run, or lift the babies. Roma was two and a half, and Randy was seven months. And I had a husband who was an invalid. It looked like I was going to have to be the primary source of financial support for the family for a while.

That was the only time in my life that Quentin ever asked me what I thought we should do. Usually, we did whatever he wanted.

I told Quentin that I thought we both needed to return to school and get him qualified for a vocation that would not be detrimental to his health. Quentin bellyached that we couldn't afford it. I dug deep into my memory and quoted Mother by saying: "We can do anything that we want if we work hard enough for it."

I went to the school principal and asked what I needed to do to get a job teaching. I had the two years of college in Texas, but not enough credits in general education to qualify for a teaching certificate. I had to change my major from straight music to music education so that I could get a provisional certificate to teach school.

The school principal told me that if I were willing to come to summer school and take nine class hours over the summer, they would add them to what I had already earned and that would be enough to qualify for a provisional teaching certificate and a job in the fall. I said, "Okay, count me in!"

I completed the nine class hours that summer, and they hired me to teach at an all-black school. They were worried about that because I was from Texas, and they thought I might be prejudice against black people. I told them, "I have never been around blacks at all, so how could I be prejudiced?" So, they said okay. I loved those little kids.

I taught from eight in the morning until noon. Quentin and I attended college together after that at Nevada Southern. I still needed to complete my degree to get a teaching certificate. It has a big campus now, but at the time, all the classes were taught in the high school. But we discovered they didn't offer all the classes we needed to get our degree. So, we would either have had to go to Reno or move to Wyoming where I could teach with just my provisional teaching certificate.

That's how we landed in Laramie. A friend of Quentin's from Texas was now teaching in Wyoming and told me just to mention his name, and I'd get a job. So, I did that, and it didn't do a lick of good!

I remember back when I was eight years old, Mother was trying to get a job teaching and we went to apply at a farmhouse way out in the country. She took me with her, and I vividly recall an old farmer in overalls came out and wiped his mouth on his sleeve. He didn't even ask us to get out of the car. He just said, in his southern accented, scratchy voice, "Whatcha waaan?" Mother said, "I understand you need a teacher and I'd like to apply for the teaching job."

The farmer saw me sitting in the car and said: "We don't haarr married women."

Mother told him that she was a widow. And he said, "You have children; we don't hire married women!" And that was it. He turned around and walked off. I wanted to hop out of that car and kick him in the shins.

That incident came back to haunt me when I got to Laramie, Wyoming, in 1956 and applied for a teaching job. In the same scratchy, southern-accented voice as the man that wouldn't even consider my mother for employment, the superintendent of the school I wanted to work for said, "We don't haarr married women." Twenty years later, those were the very same words the farmer told Mother!

Instead of teaching in Laramie, I looked for a place like a ranch that hired one person to instruct all the children on the ranch. I found a job in Bosler, Wyoming, which is twenty miles north of Laramie. I taught there the first school year we lived in Wyoming, 1956-1957. My salary was $3,000 for the year.

Quentin went to school full-time. His first semester, he flunked 11 of the 15 class hours he took. I could never imagine failing anything. I couldn't believe it! That was the closest I came to wanting to shoot him! But I didn't (Not then. Not until I shot him with a camera 20 years later).

The next school year, Quentin's friend, who lived in Walden, Colorado, told us about a school that was nine miles north of Walden in Cowdrey, Colorado that needed teachers. They didn't have a place for the teachers to stay, so they built an apartment on the back of the school building for us, and both Quentin and I taught. He taught grades 5-8, and I taught grades 1-4, and piano lessons after school. A lady right next to the school took care of our two children for us. With no commute, it was a very short day for us, so we took correspondence courses and added additional credits toward our degree.

It was an incredible year. I enjoyed it so much. At noontime, we would take all the children from the school down to the river to go ice skating. Could you imagine doing something like that today? We also flooded the playground with ice and had an ice skating rink right there on the playground.

We realized, however, that Quentin would never get his degree if we stayed in Cowdrey because he couldn't get summer courses for the classes he needed to graduate. We decided to return to Laramie, live in our camper trailer, and complete our degrees in one year rather than drag it out for years and years. I switched back to straight music again and wound up with a double major in music and musical education. That's when I started studying piano seriously.

I went back to the ranch school in Bosler, and we lived in Laramie at the student trailer park. The children slept in the bunk above our bed, each with their head at one end and their feet in the middle. Quentin and I graduated at the same time, in 1959 from the University of Wyoming.

Quentin got a job teaching High School in Lander, Wyoming after he graduated. We moved to the town that would be our home for the next 21 years (1959-1980). I had saved a small nest egg totaling a little over $800, and we used it as a down payment on a house. They required $1500 but they let us pay $800, and I taught school for half days our first year to pay the other $700. I thought it was a mansion. It was just a little frame house with three tiny bedrooms and one bath. It had a living room and a kitchen and a small utility room. It was heaven, especially compared to the camper trailer we had been living in.

I started my home studio then and taught my piano students there. We lived in that small frame home for seven years until the twins were three-years-old. In 1966 we had outgrown the frame house, and it was time to move. Quentin was campaigning for a new airplane, but I suggested we move to a more prestigious part of town, which appealed to his ego. That is when we moved into what I considered my dream home, a charming brick house a block from the park on the south side of town.

As an aside, that little house in town produced many memories for me. My piano teaching studio was in the basement of the house, and there was a fireplace down there that we used to warm up the room suitable for teaching in the winter. Every summer the family would take a trip out to the forest and cut firewood. We would cut down standing dead trees, and they were often quite unstable—even dangerous. One time when we were out there, Randy ran under a tree just as it was falling. I was scared to death! I was sure that tree would land on him. I was so relieved to see him wriggle out of danger unscathed.

Our teaching salaries were not much at that time, and we were always trying to fit continuing education into the budget. We did whatever we could to survive. In the summertime, the children and I would pick green beans from a nearby farmer's fields. We would pick "on the halves," which is a phrase that means that the farmer would keep ½ of whatever we picked, and we could take the other half home. I would can our share of the green beans we picked for use throughout the rest of the year.

I would also buy bushels of fruit such as peaches, pears, and plums from the produce trucks that would haul the fruits from Utah and sell them for $3-$4 a bushel, and can the fruit as well. I always kept a record of what I canned and one year I canned over 300 jars of fruit and vegetables for us to eat throughout the year.

The pressure cooker that my Mother used when I was a child was the perfect food processor for canning. I still have that cooker to this day. I don't can in the same quantities I once did, but if I have leftover produce from my garden that I can't finish, I will still can the excess.

When preparing food for canning, the fruit is not to be pressurized but instead given a hot water bath. I remember one time the children and I were canning peaches together. We were all in the kitchen and Roy, being the inquisitive child that he was (he was around seven years' old at this time), screwed the valve down that caused the cooker to go into pressure. None of the other children or I knew that Roy had inadvertently turned on the pressure. As we were working away, all of a sudden, the pressure in the cooker expanded and exploded with a huge hiss. We all scattered! Luckily, Quentin, who was home at the time, had the presence of mind to turn the breaker off so that the electric cooker would stop. After the danger was over, we all got quite a chuckle over that!

Another thing I did to conserve money was to make all my and the children's clothes. In those days, there was no such thing as Goodwill or Thrift stores or Garage Sales, so I had to make our clothes. I got to be quite handy at sewing, and my children seemed to love to challenge me!

I remember when Roma was attending college in Laramie, she came home one Friday for Easter break. We had never received new clothes for Easter as many people do, but that year Roma suggested we make some new Easter clothes for the kids. She was very maternal towards Ronda and the twins, probably because she was so much older than they were. She considered them her babies.

So, the Friday before Easter, we went to the store and bought fabric for the twins, Ronda and me. In two days, I made a lined suit, with jacket and pants, for Roy, and a matching pleated skirt and lined jacket for Ree, a dress and lined cape for Ronda, and a dress for me too. We all wore our new clothes to Easter Sunday church. Making all those clothes in a single weekend was quite a challenge.

Maybe it was seeing how hard we had to work to survive, or maybe it was a desire to have a little spending money of their own, but when the twins, Roy and Ree, were 11 Roy decided that he wanted to have a paper route. Ree couldn't be outdone and wanted in on it. If hired, they would have to deliver the Denver Post every morning at 5:00 AM to customers in our neighborhood, regardless of the cold. And it could sure get cold in Lander, Wyoming! I told them that it was going to be their paper route. I was not going to do it for them. They would have to commit to it.

That winter, every day I would look at the indoor/outdoor thermometer that we had in the bedroom and check it. If it was 25 degrees below zero or warmer, they had to deliver the papers on their own. If it was 26 degrees below zero or colder, they could wake up their dad or brother, and one of them would drive them on their route. It had to be 26 degrees below zero before they were allowed to have any help.

They did it every single day. I would wake them at 5:00 and they never argued a bit. They did their paper route, and when they came back, I would have a hot breakfast waiting for them. It may sound very cruel in today's standards, but we provided them with warm clothes and boots to go out into the cold as they learned to be loyal, dedicated, and committed to a goal. They got lots of tips from their customers too! People were so amazed at how devoted they were to their jobs. My kids were very responsible, and when they committed to something, they had to go through with it, and they did it. They delivered papers until we moved from town to acreage outside of Lander.

Returning to the story of my quest for a complete education, a few years after Quentin and I bought our cozy house in Lander, in 1960, Quentin decided he wanted to get his master's degree. Fortunately, he got a math scholarship from the University at Laramie in Wyoming. He wasn't good at math at all, but he managed to get that scholarship, so he headed to Laramie for the summer so that he could go to school. I stayed in Lander with Roma and Randy because I was pregnant with Ronda that summer. Quentin flunked out of the math course of study. So, he didn't continue. Ronda was born in October of that year.

Then he decided he wanted to do it again. He did his research and determined he wanted to go to Tucson, Arizona. We packed up Roma, Randy, and the baby Ronda in the summer of 1961 and went to Tucson, only for him to take one look at the campus and decide he did not like it. So, we turned around and returned to Laramie, where we stayed in our camper trailer again. While we were in Laramie, I took six credit hours of classes as well.

The summer after the twins were born, in 1962, my mother had to have surgery on her feet, and I took all the kids to Texas while Quentin went to Laramie to start an arts master's degree. The course was two sessions of five weeks each. Well, he got frustrated and quit, using an excuse that they wanted him to do modern art, and he wasn't interested in that. That was twice he'd started a master's degree and didn't continue.

But Quentin didn't want to go to school in Laramie anymore, either. So, he did his research and decided Moscow, Idaho was the place to be. We went to Moscow, Idaho in the summer of 1964. Roma was 11, Randy, 9, Ronda, 3 and Roy and Ree were 2.

I wanted to study piano with one of the professors at the University while we were in Moscow. But to take piano training, I had to be enrolled in the master's course. I told them that I couldn't do that because I had five children. The counselor said I got my bachelor's degree and taught school and piano, why can't I get my master's degree as well? Why indeed? So, I studied piano and took classes toward my master's degree. Quentin watched the kids while I was in class and I'd take over while he went.

We returned to Idaho the following summer. Surprise, surprise, Quentin flunked out of his classes for the third time. But I had two summers of classes and those six credits I had gotten at the University of Wyoming in Laramie.

All I needed to get my master's degree was to do my recital and to take a few classes the following summer. I couldn't go. There was no way I could take all the children and complete my courses and recital training as well. Quentin wasn't going to help; not when he had failed at the same goal so many times. I skipped taking classes in Idaho that summer.

For many years, Lander participated in a Community Concert Series as part of their cultural program, and they hosted musicians from all over the world. They asked me to perform a special concert as part of that series, which was a fantastic experience for me. Teaching piano is never the same as performing, and I enjoyed preparing my repertoire for the concert.

The following summer, a woman from Lander told me she wanted to go to Idaho and take a few classes, and Mother offered to care for the three little ones if I wanted to go back and complete my degree.

I thought oh boy, this is going to be a hard sell to Quentin. He didn't want me to get my master's degree because he never got his. And he was reluctant to let me do anything on my own anyway. Quentin would give his consent to things, and then he would throw it back in my face when I did it. He was working all summer for the Bureau of Land Management and wouldn't have seen us anyway.

But I did it. I took the three youngest, who were five and six years old, to Mothers, and sent Randy to spend the summer at a ranch with some friends. Roma and the woman who wanted to go to school went with me, and we pulled the camper trailer 1000 miles from Lander to Moscow.

We stayed in that camper all summer while I went to school. Roma attended band camp and took private piano lessons. I took my classes and got my master's degree. I did it! That was the summer of 1967 when I finally finished. It was THEN that I began to realize that I was as good as anybody else when it came to teaching. I finally decided that I was okay. I still had moments of inadequacy, even after I moved to Denver, but when I accomplished my goal and received my master's degree in piano performance, I started to feel like I could contend with other people.

Key #81: If your goal is important enough, keep your dream alive and figure out a way to achieve it, no matter what (or who) tries to deflate your passion along the way.

CHAPTER 17 – INVESTING MONEY FOR THE FUTURE

I had a lot of financial struggle in my life. I enjoyed most of my life; I loved my family, I loved my children. We had a great time. But financial worries were part of a significant portion of my life. Nowadays, it is beautiful not to have to worry about money.

I had no retirement account because I was self-employed for so much of my life. Even though I was frugal, I found it difficult to build a nest egg for the future. When I started receiving social security in 1995, I decided to save it all and start buying rental properties.

I had almost paid for my home, and I started thinking I needed a tax deduction. I considered a rental property might be the way to go. I talked to my husband, Buddy, about it, and initially, he wasn't in favor of it. But I thought maybe a rental property could act as a retirement fund for me if I owned a home and collected rental income from it.

So, Buddy and I started looking at property and thinking about the possibility. I had a friend who had owned a rental condo for some years. I asked her whether it worked out for her; if it were something she would recommend.

She said her condo had been an excellent investment for her, but she was thinking of selling it because she and her husband wanted to invest in some farm property. She asked if I was interested in buying her condo and I told her I didn't know.

Well, she hadn't talked to her family yet, so she said she would let me know what they decided.

One day my friend told me they had decided to sell. Did I want it? I said yes. Buddy was still not for it, but I suggested that we use it as a test. If it went smoothly, we would know it was for us. If we started having a lot of trouble, we could back off and sell it. So, we agreed to buy the condo.

A friend of mine from Lander was moving to Denver and asked if we happened to know a place for rent. I said, "It just so happens that I am in the process of buying a condo I'd be renting, but the deal has not yet closed." She said "well tell me about it." I described the condo as having three bedrooms, two baths, with an open concept living area and a garage. She said, "I'll take it!" She moved in and was there for eight years. I was able to pay the loan off over that time.

After that rental was so successful, Ronda and her husband had moved to Denver and were looking for a place. Buddy had passed away by this time, and I was hoping they would find a place close to me. But there was nothing here at that time. Ronda wanted to invest the money they had in something quickly before they spent it on something else.

She and I went to look at First Creek Farm which was a new development on Tower and 56th, just past Green Mountain Ranch, located north of metro Denver. It was beautiful. Ronda decided she wanted to buy a home there, and I said, "Well, then I will buy one too." They are exactly alike, except hers is on the northwest side and mine is on the southeast side of the same building. There are three bedrooms, two baths, open concept living area and garage.

The housing bubble of 2008 hit, and we were suddenly losing money on our investment homes. Ronda was worried that we had made a bad investment, but somehow, I was able to stay cool and assure her that as long as we keep the homes, we'd be okay. Today, those properties are worth about 1 ½ times what we paid for them, and I am expecting the value to increase even more with the new Gaylord Hotel and Convention Center going up near the airport. My property is paid in full

Key #82: Don't let fear talk you into cashing in your investments early. Believe in your long-term goals.

Becoming debt free has become an essential focus in my life. I don't run up credit card debt. My main home is paid for. When I get a loan for an investment home, getting the loan paid off is on the top of my priority list. I think three things are foolish financial investments. They include:

- Making late payments and incurring additional fees.
- Writing insufficient funds checks and having to pay the costs incurred by them.
- Allowing credit card interest to compound.

All those things eat up money for no reason.

I've outgrown several things in my life. Ironing, animals, husbands and debt!

My first two investment homes had Homeowner's Association (HOA) fees. They didn't bother me at first, but they always go up. You have no control, the Homeowner's Association can raise the price at will, and it keeps going up. Every time the fees go up, my profit on the property goes down.
When I bought my third rental property, I decided I didn't want a related HOA. There was a house in my neighborhood about two blocks from me. It was a ranch, which is a favorite style for rental homes. It has a full basement, three bedrooms, and three baths. When I looked at it, the market was low, and I got it for a reasonable price.

I put a property manager in charge of my two condos in 2005. Her name is Beth Gillard, and she was recommended to me by my banker. She has been fabulous. She collects the rent and takes out 10% of what she receives. I get the remaining 90%. If something breaks, she lets me know. I don't even know who is renting the properties anymore. She does it all. I get checks in the mail.

The reason I hired Beth in the first place was because of a bad experience I had with a tenant in my first condo. There was a gal who was supposed to be a Christian, who had a teenaged daughter. I felt sorry for her because she had just gotten a divorce. I had even given her $500 before she moved in, out of the goodness of my heart because I felt sorry for her. Then she moved into my place, and she paid the rent one time. The rest of the time she lived there, which was close to two years, she never gave me the full amount. She would pay $50 or $200, but she never paid the total rent. So, that is when I hired Beth because I had never had anything like that happen before and I didn't want it to happen again.

I would highly recommend that if you choose to buy a rental property, that you get a property manager unless you are a handyman that can fix everything and you want to handle the renters. I chose to manage the house in my neighborhood for five years before turning it over to Beth. I finally realized I needed her for that property as well.

For the first five years, I had a mother and two daughters living in the ranch home, and they were great. I didn't need a property manager. I had no problem collecting the rent from them. But when they moved out, I got a series of tenants that gave me nothing but trouble.

The first tenants moved out in a month, and the family that came after them sweet talked me into cutting down the security deposit and insisted on me installing an air conditioner. Then they told me, after they had moved in, that the people who lived in my house before them had cats and that their son was ill because of the cats. They didn't want to pay the rent, and they were going to sue me because I rented the house in an uninhabitable condition. They kept living in the house but said it was uninhabitable. They wouldn't move out. I had to have them evicted, and they owed two month's rent. When I finally got them removed, they stole the washer and dryer from the basement. After that experience, I decided that I needed Beth to take care of that property too.

Despite the disappointing experiences with some of my tenants, I would recommend investing in rental property. But I highly recommend getting a property manager like Beth. She is the fortress between the renters and me. I don't have to have anything to do with the renters. I don't deal with their personalities, and they don't know who I am. Without the buffer of a property manager, it is too easy for a renter to take advantage of you.

Key #83: Do what you do best and hire the rest.

One of the reasons I am so thankful for my financial success is that I can contribute to the charitable causes I believe in. I send money every month to my daughter, Ree, and her husband Alan in Brazil to help pay for their missionary efforts. I contribute to the Mountain States Children's Home. I spend money for the program In Search Of the Lord's Way every month. I help a family here in town by supplying them with free Juice Plus. And I support a couple that travels in their motor home throughout the country providing interim ministerial care for congregations when their ministers need to be absent.

It is important to me to help people do what God wants them to do. So, by sending money to Brazil, it's not for my daughter and son in law to live on, it's to help with their work teaching people about the Bible. That's why I support the charities I choose. I'm thankful I can do it. I have never been able to do things like that before. At first, I just gave to my congregation. But as I've made more money I have been able to give more. And, that is a great feeling to be able to do.

Key #84: God has a bigger shovel than I do. I shovel it out; he shovels it in.

CHAPTER 18 – IT'S ALL ABOUT FAMILY

For me, succeeding at any challenge or meeting any goal is empty without my family nearby to share it. As a young family, my children and I spent a lot of time together working, performing, and we fit some play in there too!

In 1976, for example, we took a canoe and kayak trip with friends that had three children around the same ages as Ronda, Ree, and Roy. We drifted and rowed by water from Fontenelle Dam to Green River, Wyoming, over four days and never saw another human the whole time. We adults stayed in the two canoes, and the six children took turns with the two kayaks. No one flipped over the entire trip! It was so peaceful. I don't recall seeing any other people but our group the entire trip.

We would float down the river and see moose and elk and all kinds of wildlife coming down the hills to the waterside to drink. We slept out under the stars in sleeping bags on the shoreline, and we all just had a wonderful time. Even Quentin was on his best behavior, probably because we were with friends and he didn't want them to think negatively of him.

Quentin brought a guitar, and of course, we sang a lot during the trip! We took no pictures, and I did not journal our activities of that trip, so the only record I have of those four days is in my memory.

Quentin was an outdoorsman and enjoyed teaching the children how to start campfires and catch fish. I was in charge of supplying and cooking all the food, as always. And, as required, I made fresh biscuits and gravy daily for breakfast.

Quentin, the kids and I made our canoe out of wood and coated it with fiberglass. It was beautiful; we did excellent work. They had a lot of fun building that canoe and my son, Randy, was a bit upset with me when I sold it years later for only $100. In fact, Roy builds kayaks and races them today. His interest in kayaking started way back then in 1976.

Another fond memory of a family trip was a 40-mile backpacking trip in 1973 from Dickenson Park in Wyoming over the Continental Divide to Pinedale, Wyoming. Quentin decided one day we would make the hike. I never got a say in where we would go for family outings. Since he was a teacher, he had the summer off and could easily schedule things for us to do without much warning or planning.

It was an especially memorable trip for the children. We had a donkey named Hannibal who carried a lot of our gear, and we spent two weeks on the trip. I loved sitting around the campfire each night and talking about the events of the day. While we talked, I wrote the details in a journal each night, and when I told my children I was working on this book, they insisted my complete journal of the 13-day trip be included. Those daily accounts have been added to the back of this book as a sort of virtual getaway from the modern-day hustle and bustle.

I strongly recommend journaling your trips because you do not realize at the time how much you will forget later. Describing one trip from memory and another using my actual journal will show the difference in details and should support my advice to journal.

I am blessed with a close family that has grown rather large with grandchildren and great-grandchildren. A primary reason I work so hard to stay healthy is to give me as much time as I can with my dear family.

That is why our bi-annual family reunion is of number one importance to me. They started in 1986. The kids and I were together for what seemed like the last time for a while because Ree and Alan were moving to Brazil to become missionaries, and Roy was graduating and going into the military. We had gathered together for Roy's graduation and commissioning.

One night when we were all together visiting, I said: "Okay kids, this is it. Everybody's leaving, and this is the first time we will be separated. And we don't know when we will see each other again unless we make plans. I hope you will all come to see me now and then, but you won't see each other unless we plan it. Do you want to be like most other families and just see each other sporadically? Would you like your future children to know their aunts and uncles and cousins?"

They all agreed they wanted to get together intentionally and the Roberts Family Reunion was born.

Ree and Alan return to the US every two years on furlough, so we agreed that we would plan the reunion around their return. Our first reunion was in 1988, and we have been together every two years since then. Those homecomings are some of my most cherished memories.

Until 1998, we met at my house. By then, the family had grown, and it was too crowded. That year we went to Snow Mountain Ranch in the Colorado Mountains, and it was fabulous. We've gone to Palm Springs, California, Buchanan Lake, in Texas, Jasper, Missouri, and Sedalia, Colorado. Sedalia is a family favorite because we can rent a huge house that fits everybody. These past few reunions we have scheduled at Buchanan Lake in Texas so my brother James, who is in his nineties and resides in Texas, can attend without heavy travel.

Our reunions go from Wednesday noon until Saturday noon. I know a lot of people dread attending family reunions, but my kids don't feel that way. Maybe some of the in-laws get a bit less excited about our get-togethers, but not my kids! They love it, and the little ones love it. I remember one of my grandchildren asking me why we only have our reunions every two years. He didn't like to wait and told me he wished they could be every year. It is heart-warming to see that they enjoy it so much!

We have the same menu every time. I always make hot biscuits from scratch every morning like we did when the kids were living at home. We have bacon and eggs or oatmeal, but we never skip the biscuits and gravy!

Wednesday night, we have Mexican food. We have enchiladas and tostadas. We prepare tostadas differently than you would see in a restaurant.

Thursday we always cook a big Thanksgiving-style turkey dinner. For a while, our reunions were arranged around Thanksgiving time, and we got into the habit of having a big celebration with turkey and all the trimmings. Few people miss reunion dinner on Thursday night!

On Friday we keep it simple with leftovers, snacks and maybe a pasta dish.

Most people are surprised to discover that television is off limits during our reunion weekend because the focus is on being together with each other. We made a rule that nobody is to watch TV during our reunion events. Instead, we play a lot of games like Mexican Train and Rummikub. We always have a big 1,000-piece puzzle we work on throughout the weekend. One year one of the kids brought a 3D puzzle, and we started making those. We assembled the White House! It was beautiful.

And, not surprisingly with our music background, we sing a

lot. We have songbooks with our favorite songs so everyone has a copy and can sing along. There is always a talent show during our reunions, usually on Friday night, before we all have to depart the next day. Every family participates in the talent show. Little kids might showcase the instruments they're learning at school. One family might offer a skit, telling a joke or demonstrating a juggling routine. I'm always impressed at the variety and talent displayed by all.

I have assembled several photo albums with pictures of past reunions, and everyone enjoys paging through those albums and reminiscing.

In general, we do most reunion activities as a group, be it hiking, or boating or swimming. The goal is to be together for three days. I love those times. We have so much fun, and everyone is together and talking about old times. I learn more about what my kids did when they were young than I ever knew at the time. They will tell stories of things they did when they were young, and I will be just astounded that I missed them when they happened in real-time.

It has been remarkable that almost everyone attends our family reunions every time they are offered. There have been only a few exceptions. It helps that we only plan three days, and we try to divide up the costs equitably so that it is not too significant a burden on any one family. My two remaining brothers started joining us in 1998. Harold has passed away now, but James will be 91 when we get together this summer 2018.

And Charles' daughter, Carol Ann is coming to the reunions now as well. When Harold died, in 1988, Carol Ann saw the obituary and attended the funeral. Her stepdad had just died two weeks before, and she wanted to connect with the family again. We had grown apart after Charles' memorial service. But Carol Ann had no remaining relatives, and so we welcomed her back to our family.

I sometimes wonder if the reunions will continue after I'm gone. I don't think the family would have remained this close if we didn't get together so regularly. The kids seem willing to make it happen. It will be up to them when I'm not around. But I hope that is not for many years to come.

Key #85: Schedule multi-day events with your family. Then, journal your activities so that you can enjoy remembering the details for years to come.

CHAPTER 19: SWITCHING GEARS
TO A NEW GOAL

In 2014 I retired after 74 years of teaching piano. It was a difficult decision because teaching had been such a rewarding and consuming part of my life for all those years. I was honored to receive Colorado Music Teacher of the Year and the National Teacher's Association Fellow of the Year. The public recognition I received from my colleagues when they presented me with those awards felt terrific. I loved the children; I loved the parents; I loved the music; I loved almost everything about it.

Except, I hated the scheduling. I scheduled my students for the September – August year in July and August. It was always a nightmare, fitting everyone into both a group and a personal lesson slot that met my program goals and the student's calendar. In April of that year, the temptation to avoid going through the scheduling ordeal was too great to ignore.

I decided that with my rental property investments and the residual income I have built up with Juice Plus, which I know will continue to grow, that I had enough money to live on without teaching piano. And I was having some trouble with my eyes that made it difficult to read and play music, which is a significant consideration for a piano teacher. So, I just decided that it was time.

Most of my students were stunned. The three that were going to be seniors that year were devastated. They felt as though I had abandoned them. They begged me to work with them for just one more year, through graduation. I finally agreed to give the three seniors private lessons, but no group lessons or recitals. But it didn't work out. Without the benefit of my planned program that included group lessons and performances as motivation, they did not put in the effort to increase their skills. They did not work up to the level they had done in the past at all. I threatened and cajoled, but that last year wasn't gratifying for them as students or me as the teacher.

Key #86: When it is time for something to end and a new chapter to begin, make the change entirely.

I have thoroughly enjoyed the freedom of not having to be at my house at a specific time every day, every week. It has been very freeing. It gives me the opportunity to spread my wings, see new possibilities and set new goals for my life. When I retired at age 84, when many people shut the book on their future, mine had just begun anew!

My new purpose is to look good, feel good, make money, and have fun. I wear a bracelet every day that has that principle inscribed. Juice Plus is the vehicle I intend to use to power my purpose.

As I've shared, I was a hard nut to crack at first. I was not an evangelist for Juice Plus from day one. My friend had to persuade and even coerce me to try Juice Plus and then later to attend my first conference. Now, I plan to get to the top of the company and help a lot of people along the way. I've learned that the secret to success is to offer people an option, just like my friend provided the opportunity to me. Whether they follow through on the choice presented is up to them, just like it was up to me.

Key #87: Do not be afraid to offer people the option you have chosen.

Having a driving force makes all the difference in the world. I laughed at Roma way back when for saying she didn't care about the money and she just wanted to play with the symphony. I understand her opinion much better now. My life experiences, and most recently my ventures with Juice Plus, have led me to realize that money is rarely the prize. It's our driving force that keeps us going. At first, with Juice Plus, my drive was a belief in the product and the money-making potential. It is hard to discount the motivation of medical benefits and the residual income possibilities that are there for someone in my family from my Juice Plus business when I am gone.

But, in the end, the money is no longer what drives me to grow in the Juice Plus business. What I want to do now is to help as many people in the world as I can to become more healthy, wealthy and wise. And my goal to achieve that is to get high enough up the Juice Plus organization that I am asked to present to thousands and thousands of future Juice Plus entrepreneurs at conferences. That is my driving force.

Key #88: Money is wonderful, but it isn't the end prize.

Back Row: Buddy, Randy, Allen
Next Row: Jonathan, Shane, Roy, Hazel
Next Row: Roma, Ronda, Jan
Next: Ree holding Natalie, Joash, Lynnsey,
Tanya holding Daniel
Jara, Nathanael

TO BE CONTINUED!

Mother was adamant about proper grammar and diction from the time I was very young. I remember her enrolling me in elocution lessons when I was five years old. I would be assigned readings that I needed to memorize and recite with correct enunciation, pronunciation, and diction. Those early lessons made me acutely aware of people's speech and articulation.

I wonder what Mother would think of this book if she had the opportunity to read it before her passing. Would she gloss over the stories and focus on specific words I chose to use to describe certain sentences or people? Would she read the stories remembering her involvement to be different than what my descriptions have provided? What if my first husband, Quentin, read it? Would he feel any remorse or guilt?

What if my father could read what became of his little girl? Would he focus on my financial struggles or successes? Would he be angry at Quentin for his leaving me for another woman or be happy for me for the time I spent with Buddy? I would have liked to get to know him before he died. I think he would have been proud of me. He surely would have been proud of my brothers and children as well.

I hope that my family reads this book and refers to it often as they move through different segments of their lives for years to come. I have devoted my life to providing for my family. And, this book is an example of that commitment. There is no greater act of love than to revisit the minute details of one's life and construct the important lessons learned in a way that one's descendants can benefit from. My family is my driving force.

If I have one bonus key to offer, I would suggest the importance of identifying your driving force. Whatever your plans are now, or become later, you can only make plans for how to achieve your goals when you know what your driving force is.

For example, I never took a speech class in high school or college. I knew the moment I set the goal to advance high enough in the Juice Plus business to speak to thousands of people at their conferences that I needed to be able to present my ideas well. I decided that Toastmasters was where I needed to be so that I would be ready when the time came for me to speak for Juice Plus audiences.

I was 84 years old when I joined Toastmasters, a worldwide non-profit organization dedicated to the ongoing learning and practice for people wanting to improve their communication and leadership skills. I remember that day vividly. I announced to the group at the beginning of the meeting that I had completed the form and paid my club membership dues. Everyone applauded and welcomed me in as a new member.

At the end of the same meeting, the founder of our club stood up and announced that, since he was 84, he was going to retire from the club. He was quitting because he is 84, and I was beginning at age 84!

Most people expect to get old. Society tells them that is what they are supposed to do, and they follow the norm. I remember when I was younger, people would say "act your age" when someone was having too much fun or being childish. I don't know if I ever did act my age. When I was young, I worked harder in the cotton fields than many of the adults did. Now that I have reached "retirement," I am having so much more fun and enjoying such achievement than most people my age.

And so, this seems like a great place to stop my story for now.

You won't be getting any concluding words from me. I am not a fan of conclusions. I have never been. Every conclusion ushers in a new beginning, and that is certainly the case in my life and yours.

I'll merely end for now by saying: Mother was right. You really can do anything you want, as long as you want it badly enough. I'd like to add to her message by suggesting, "All you have to do is keep playing the M.U.S.I.C."

Until the next story begins,

Love, Hazel

HAZEL RAMSBOTHAM

APPENDIX 1:
COMPLETE LIST OF 88 KEYS

1. You really can do anything you want in life, as long as you want it badly enough, (plus my addition to the saying) even when surprises try to convince you otherwise.
2. Some things need to be done without complaint.
3. Avoiding pain motivates everyone to act.
4. Your family is in it together.
5. Be satisfied with what you have.
6. We know that God causes everything to work together for the good of those who love God and are called according to his purpose for them. (Romans 8:28 NLT)
7. God will take care of us if we trust and behave according to His will.
8. Pay attention to the things for which you are passionate about.
9. Trust yourself to do the best job you can.
10. Follow where God leads you.
11. Seek advice but be willing to decide against that advice.
12. Don't compare yourself to anyone else. Focus on being the best you can be.
13. Allow others to believe in you until you can believe in yourself.
14. Let the positive energy of a group propel you forward when you can't do it on your own.

15. Fear God and obey his commands, for this is everyone's duty.
16. Be your own underwriter. No one wants it as much as you do.
17. Don't be afraid to work hard for what you want.
18. Don't allow the motivations of others to keep you from achieving your goals.
19. Never marry for anything but love.
20. Don't let guilt hold you back from your dreams.
21. Suffering produces endurance, and endurance produces character, and character produces hope (Romans 5: 3-4 NLT)
22. Look for the good in everyone, even if you have to look deep.
23. You never know who you are making an impression on, so always act in a way that will leave a good impression.
24. Loyalty is a two-way street.
25. Do what you need to do to correct a bad situation. If you choose not to act, be prepared and content to put up with the results.
26. Making tough decisions for an aging parent is not easy for anyone. Seek advice from others, but let your heart make the final decision.
27. Show compassion to people, even if you have differences with them.
28. You are the captain of your circumstances.
29. Some secrets are okay to tell others.
30. Selling anything is easy when you know how much it will help the person who needs it.
31. Don't judge a people by its place.
32. Things have a way of working out the way they are supposed to. Be open to opportunities, and you'll be surprised at what happens.
33. Embrace your desires and go for it, unafraid.
34. Prevention is better than cure. Don't blindly rely on your doctor to make you healthy.

35. Your health is your wealth. Adopt an exercise program from someone you trust and do it every day.

36. Never allow someone to make you go crazy just because they are.

37. Meditate on God's directions and ask Him for help.

38. Your family is your greatest blessing.

39. Your family needs you to be firm, but fair.

40. You can foster the habit of your children getting along with each other and being happy with each other, or you can instill the habit of constant fighting. Which will it be?

41. The inmates don't run the asylum. Run your family the same way.

42. "Happiness belongs to the self-sufficient." - Aristotle

43. Accept the unexpected. It can bring happiness even if you are not looking for it.

44. People can't change time but time changes people.

45. Travel nurtures an adventuresome spirit. Better to see something than to just hear or read about it.

46. Even if you aren't searching for something, be ready to welcome it into your life when it finds you.

47. Honesty brings honor to those you love.

48. Connect with others, and they will send opportunity your way.

49. Even people you trust can be unpredictable. Trust your instinct, but with a watchful eye.

50. Even if you've been burned many times, someone will always come along to provide an improved situation, if you are open to it.

51. Be brave enough to stand your ground when you need to.

52. Be thankful for where you live and for what you have. There is always someone who would love to have what you have.

53. Learn from the people around you and expect that they are learning from you.

54. Even in unfortunate times, there are positive

memories that are worth keeping with you forever.

55. Stick up for yourself and your family when you need to.
56. When enough is enough, that is enough!
57. Try not to cry over someone that hurts you. They don't deserve your tears.
58. Crying is not the only way to feel better.
59. Know how you want to be treated and insist on it.
60. Beware of false help.
61. When hiring people for professional services, oversee their every move to assure you are getting the services you paid for.
62. When you have done everything you can, and things still are not in your favor, move on.
63. Be thankful and aware of the people who are on your side.
64. Trust your decisions.
65. Get mad when it is time to get mad.
66. People are just people.
67. God isn't prejudiced. Why should we be?
68. Find people's needs and fulfill them.
69. Even in times of diversity, expect at least some things to fall into place. Be grateful when those times happen.
70. People might doubt what you say but have to believe what you do.
71. Sometimes breaking the rules is the right thing to do.
72. Honor your grief.
73. Life is for the living.
74. When you need to get over something, get busy with your life.
75. Try three times before asking for help.
76. The second you stop playing, it quits being music. So, don't ever stop playing.
77. The world is not going to coddle you. Learn from your setbacks.
78. Introduce children to music very early in life.

79. When you lose your desire to improve, you may as well be dead.

80. Talent isn't enough. You need hard work to reap success.

81. If your goal is important enough, keep your dream alive and figure out a way to achieve it, no matter what (or who) tries to deflate your passion along the way.

82. Don't let fear talk you into cashing in your investments early. Believe in your long-term goals.

83. Do what you do best and hire the rest.

84. God has a bigger shovel than I do. I shovel it out; he shovels it in.

85. Schedule multi-day events with your family. Then, journal your activities so that you can enjoy remembering the details for years to come.

86. When it is time for something to end and a new chapter to begin, make the change entirely.

87. Do not be afraid to offer people the option you have chosen.

88. Money is wonderful, but it isn't the end prize..

APPENDIX 2: TIMELINE

1930
Hazel Roby is born on April Fool's Day (April 1).

1936
John Charles Roby, Hazel's father, dies on January 25. Hazel is five years old. Hazel and her brothers, Harold, James, and Charles pick cotton over the next six summers. Hazel is age 6-11.

1937
Hazels learns to play piano by ear, and decides she wants to teach piano when she grows up. She is six.

1939
Hazel takes piano lessons from her teenage neighbor during the winters she is 9 and 10.

1941
Hazel begins teaching piano to neighborhood children. She is 11 and teaches for 74 more years.

1941
Hazel makes her first two quilt tops the summer she is 11.

1942
Hazel learns to crochet at age 12. Since then, she has crocheted four bedspreads, six tablecloths, and countless doilies.

1943
Hazel and her Mother live in Dallas over the summer to be near her Aunt Loreen. She learns to play the accordion. She is

13.

1944
Hazel and her Mother move from Cunningham Texas to Iowa Park Texas. Hazel is 14 and a sophomore in high school.

1945
Hazel begins teaching at the Norsworthy Music Store on Saturdays. She is 15.

1946
Hazel continues to teach at Norsworthy Music Store and adds additional hours after school when she is 16 until she graduates High School at 17 in 1947.

1947
Hazel attends Harden College in Wichita Falls, Texas on a full scholarship. She works as a student aid to the head of the music department teaching music theory.

1949
Hazel desires to attend North Texas Teachers College in Denton, Texas, for her final two years, but never attends. She marries Quentin Roberts at age 19.

1950
Hazel and Quentin live in Houston, Texas. She loses her first child to toxemia (preeclampsia).

1952
Quentin works as a Border Patrol agent in the Rio Grande area, Texas.

1953
January, Roma Ruth is born in Benito, Texas, just on the border of Mexico. Hazel is 22.

1954

Quentin quits job as Border Patrol agent and he and Hazel move to Las Vegas. Roma is 19 months and Hazel is eight months pregnant with Randall Ray. Quentin gets a job welding and in machine repair at his brother's shop.

1955

Quentin has heart trouble and has to quit his welding job.

1956

Hazel works at an all-black public school in Las Vegas and she and Quentin take classes at Nevada Southern College Las Vegas. Quentin also works as an in-house detective for the Hotel Sahara.

1957

Hazel and Quentin move to Laramie, Wyoming. Hazel is 27. She teaches in Bosler, 20 miles northwest of Laramie and Quentin attends college full time. He fails 11 of 15 credit hours the first semester.

1959

Hazel graduates with a double major (education and music) and is finally able to study music seriously with accomplished teachers. She is 29. Hazel and Quentin move to Lander, Wyoming, and Hazel starts her first home piano studio and begins building a clientele of piano students.

1960

Ronda Renee is born. Hazel is 30.

1962

The twins, Ronald Roy and Ronelda Ree are born. Hazel is 32. In the summer, 1962 Hazel takes all 5 children to Iowa Park to care for her mother who had foot surgery. Quentin attends school toward an arts master's degree, but does not complete the course.

1964

The family spends the summer in Moscow, Idaho. Quentin and Hazel attend school there.

1965

The Roberts Family Band forms and performs publicly. Hazel is 34, Roma, 11, Randall, 9, Ronda, 3 and Roy and Ree, 2. Hazel and Quentin spend a second summer in Moscow, Idaho, attending school. Quentin fails out, but Hazel only needs a few additional classes and a recital to earn her master's degree.

1967

Hazel's brother, Charles, is listed MIA (missing in action) in Vietnam. Hazel and Roma spend the summer in Moscow, Idaho, and Hazel earns her master's degree in Music Performance. She is 37.

1969

Quentin moves to Taos, New Mexico, for the summer and leaves Hazel and the kids to fend for themselves in Lander, Wyoming.

1974

The family moves from town to property just outside of Lander, Wyoming to build their dream home. The home was scheduled to be finished by fall of 1975, but never was completed.

1976

The Valentine's Day incident occurs between Hazel and Quentin, which signals the beginning of the end for their marriage.

1977

Hazel tracks Quentin and her 23-year-old piano student to a

motel 150 miles away and snaps pictures of them together. Quentin never returns home. Hazel is 47 and Quentin is 49.

1978
Hazel's brother, Charles, military status is changed from MIA to KIA (killed in action). Hazel begins working for Dynique. Randy's wife leaves Randy and his 16-month-old son, Shane, and Randy becomes a single parent.

1979
Randy moves to Denver to start his gunsmithing business and musical career. Ronda and Hazel move to Denver to work for Dynique. Hazel plans to run the Colorado/Wyoming/Utah region of Dynique. She is 49. Roy and Ree stay in Wyoming alone to finish their final year of high school.

1980
Roy and Ree graduate from high school. Dynique folds, leaving Hazel without a job and stuck with approximately $15K in cosmetic inventory. Hazel starts targeting strip clubs as a market for her cosmetics, and, eventually, jewelry as well. She also reinstates her career as a piano instructor.

1982
Randy and Ronda marry and move out of Hazel's Denver house.

1983
Hazel starts hosting foreign exchange students in her home.

1984
Hazel's mother moves to Denver to live with Hazel. Hazel is 54.

1985
June rents a room from Hazel.

1986

Roy graduates college and enters the military. Ree and her husband commit to being missionaries in Brazil. The Roberts Family Reunion is born.

1988

Hazel stops marketing to strippers. She travels to Brazil to see Ree and Alan. The first family reunion is held at Hazel's home. Mother turns 90 and moves out of Hazel's home.

1990

Hazel meets and marries Buddy. Charles' remains are returned from Vietnam and Hazel attends his military funeral at Arlington National Cemetery. June moves out amid conflict. Hazel begins training Jason Geary and does so for 3 years. Hazel is 60.

1992

Hazel's mother dies at age 93. The third family reunion is held at Hazel's home. She is 62.

1995

Hazel turns 65 and starts receiving social security benefits. She saves it and eventually invests the money in real estate rentals.

1996

The Sixth family reunion is held at Roy's home in Signal Mountain, Tennessee. Hazel travels to Vienna to visit her eldest daughter, Roma.

1997

Jara, Hazel's granddaughter, is killed in a devastating car crash.

1998

The family reunion has outgrown Hazel's home. The seventh reunion is held at Snow Mountain Ranch in the Colorado Mountains.

2000
Hazel and Buddy travel to London. The eighth family reunion is in Palm Springs.

2001
Buddy dies of a stroke at the age of 76. Hazel is 71. Hazel focuses solely on piano instruction for her livelihood at this time.

2003
Hazel has invested in two rental properties.

2005
Hazel hires a property manager, Beth Gillard, to manage her properties.

2006
Hazel awarded teacher of the year for the state of Colorado.

2010
Hazel turns 80. She is named MTNA Fellow by her peers and colleagues.

2011
Hazel travels to Egypt at the age of 81. She rides a camel!

2012
The 13th family reunion is held in Sedalia, CO. Hazel is 82. She is introduced to Juice Plus by an old friend and starts to see financial results from the business.

2014
Hazel retires from piano teaching after 74 years to pursue the Juice Plus business full time. She is 84.

2015

Hazel joins Toastmasters at the age of 84.

2017

Hazel travels to Dubai for Juice Plus grand opening, Dubai. She is 86. She attends Loren Slocum-Lahav's bootcamp in Las Vegas. Hazel also travels to her 70th high school reunion and to Manassas, VA, for her grandson's wedding.

2018

Hazel completes her book: *88 Keys to Living a Long and Purposeful Life.* The 16th Robert's family reunion is planned for Buchanan Lake, Texas in August 2016. Hazel is 88.

.

APPENDIX 3: ROBERTS FAMILY PACK TRIP (WYOMING JULY 24-AUGUST 3, 1973) – JOURNAL BY HAZEL ROBERTS

After putting Paulo Bueno, our Brazilian exchange student on the 8:00 plane in Riverton, Wyoming, we left the house at 9:30 a.m. amid the usual chaos of trying to get ready to go anywhere, especially a 12-day pack trip. We stopped by and got Gene Hunt and drove to the acre to get Hannibal, our donkey. He loaded in the back of the truck very willingly, and we set out for Dickenson Park, which was an uneventful and pleasant ride. We ate a quick, cold lunch before we put the pack saddle on Hannibal. The pack gear, though never having been assembled and loaded before, balanced and rode very well.

A week and a half prior to the trip, Hannibal had gotten badly tangled in his tether rope and severely burned his left hind foot. About one-fourth the way up from Dickenson Park to Bear's Ears Pass, he started laming up on us. We stopped and made camp at that point, since it had started to rain and Hannibal was lame. The children went off down the hill to a stream to haul some water back to camp, while we built a fire and setup a lean-to.

It rained intermittently all the rest of the afternoon, while we lay around camp trying to decide what to do about Hannibal and the pack trip. We decided to send word back to Gene Hunt to scrounge up two more back packs, and bring them to Dickenson Park. He could then take Hannibal back to the acre and we could continue our pack trip with fewer luxuries, after seriously revising our packs to accommodate eleven days' groceries.

This necessitated a trip down the mountain to the Ranger Station approximately 2 ½ miles one way, so Ronda and Dad chose to go, while Roy, Ree and Mom stayed at camp to wash supper dishes, carry more water, and improve camp conditions in general. The trip began at 6:00 and was completed at 8:15 – QUICK!

No ranger was there, but a mountaineering group from Minnesota assured dad they would relay the message to Gene Hunt, either tonight or early in the morning.

This morsel of eloquence was written at dusk, as everyone drank hot tea and roasted marshmallows over the open fire.

Earlier, as we went down for water, mom didn't notice land marks too carefully, so naturally, mom became a little confused. Mom was carrying a dishpan of water, Roy had the Dutch oven and coffee pot, and Ree had a covered pan. We had to stop a couple of times to rest, since the climb was steep. When we went far enough that we thought we should be at camp, Ree called to Hannibal and said, "Hannibal, bray for us." He promptly responded, revealing we were 50 yards to the left of the camp sight.

Mom wanted to surprise dad and Ronda with a cake in the new, 8" Dutch oven we purchased for the trip. She looked all over for a cake mix she KNEW we brought, and in looking, we discovered the pancake mix bag had been burst and was spilled all over the panier. Luckily, we had plastic bread sack with a few slices of bread in it, so we salvaged what pancake mix we could, and put it in the bread sack.

We finally found the cake mix, and mom carefully mixed half

of it, and put it in the Dutch oven, moved the grate from the fire, and set the Dutch oven right in the coals, put a few coals on top of the lid, and sat back to wait until it was done. Before we thought it had time to cook, Mom smelled something burning, so she ventured a look-see. It was burned to a crisp!
The ominous shrieks of frigidity as everyone crawled into their cold sleeping bags, and the fire slowly settled down to coals, indicated that the first day out had come to an end. We saw two pack groups today.

July 25, 1973

We weren't in too big a hurry to get up, because we knew Gene Hunt couldn't be at the ranger station too early, and we would have plenty of time to rearrange things and get there.

Ree, Roy and Dad left camp after we had breakfast, and rearranged pack gear with the idea of having Hannibal sent back to Lander. His feet looked better, but we were still apprehensive. He made the trek down the mountain carrying the pack with all the returning gear very well, and we began to wonder if he was as hurt as we had first suspected.

At the guard station, two Indians and a forest ranger affirmed that Hannibal could make the trip without any difficulty. The ranger also affirmed that the message to Gene Hunt had been relayed, and he was probably on his way.

Dad reached the conclusion that Hannibal could continue the trip, and after doctoring his feet, and eating a granola snack, they settled down to wait for Gene, who arrived shortly. He brought two friends with him because from the message he received, he didn't know whether someone had been hurt or what had happened. Charlie Smith and Connie Lain came along with two extra back packs, prepared to carry us out of the mountains. We thanked them cordially, and headed back to camp, bringing the packs so Hannibal's load could be lightened.

Back at the camp, Ronda and Mom had been cooking beans for lunch in the Dutch oven, and we all enjoyed a meal of beans, cornbread, onions, honey and topped it all off with butterscotch pudding, before beginning the long trek toward Valentine Lake.

While all was quiet, and only Mom and Ronda were at camp, an inquisitive deer ventured in closer and closer to take a look. He would rubberneck a while, then crow-hop back a short distance before succumbing to curiosity, and coming in for a closer sniff. He would gaze from a different angle each time, finally almost completely circling the camp.

Shortly after leaving the camp, we missed Piney, our dog, and although we called and called to her, she never appeared again. We remembered her leaving with us, and are wondering what could have happened to her.

We climbed and climbed, above timber line and had to take frequent rest stops, agreeing all the while that this trip wasn't for the pale hearted, or lily-livered! Each of us was carrying a heavy load in order to lighten Hannibal's, until we have him better trained, and his feet are cured. However he worked well today.

About 6:00 we made camp in a grove of much-stunted Alpine Junipers in a glacial basin lined with snow. After some finagling, we managed to scratch up enough dry wood and spread the shelter canopy. The highest trees in the vicinity were about 4 feet high.

We ate a delightful banquet meal of left-over beans, cheese, onions, dip and tortillas. No one had to be coaxed to bed tonight! We met three groups of back packers today on foot, and one on horseback.

Thursday, July 26, 1973

After a pancake breakfast, we hit the trail ad 9:05 a.m. We trudged along Lizard Head Trail for what seemed like miles, and each time we rounded a peak, we thought it would be the last before we could begin going down again. We finally surmounted the top and the view was breathtakingly beautiful. We were truly "On Top of the World, Looking Down on Creation!"

We began a welcomed descent of switchbacks, and muddy trail leading into Valentine Lake. Then it happened! Dad, who had been blessing and encouraging Hannibal, was jerked to a sudden halt. Hannibal was pinned. Having forgotten to position the rump, a strap to keep the pack saddle from going over the donkey's head in downhill motion, Dad looked around with chagrin at another equally foolish jackass who stood in a decidedly downhill position with pack saddle, cinches, paniers, Dutch oven, and a wild assortment of gear piled in a neat circular heap around his front legs!

After disassembling some of the gear, and lifting pack saddle, paniers and the rest of the gear back on Hannibal, we were able to continue our journey, making sure of course, that the rump strap was in place. We had been climbing the whole trip so far, and had almost forgotten what the rump strap was for! Each hour we stopped for a little snack of candy or granola, but on the steep climbs we would stop for a couple of minutes rest every 10 to 15 minutes.

The last three miles downhill was quite enjoyable to us all. Even Hannibal pranced along without too much coaxing. There was one problem, though. We had to put on our brakes so much our feet kept sliding to the ends of our shoes, and that made for some cramped toes.

One lake came into view, but it wasn't Valentine, so we

reluctantly trudged on until we came to Valentine Meadows, which led us to a breathtaking spectacle! Valentine is nestled in a glacial cirque with granite spires reaching up 1500 to 2,000 feet above, adorned with minor glaciers and snow fields clinging to any surface which was not vertical. The valley floor itself is covered with pine, and boulders strewn with an entertaining assortment of chipmunks everywhere.

We set about picking a camp site which offered level sleeping area, a place to tie our awning, cooking space (flat rock and place to build a fire), easy access to water, and plenty of firewood. All these qualifications were quickly met, and everyone was eager to make camp and relax after about six hours of almost constant walking.

Dad tried his hand at fishing, so we could have fish for supper, but everyone was too hungry to wait. Besides, it had been threatening to rain all afternoon, and we decided we'd better eat something else and save fishing until tomorrow. Mom wanted a fish dinner on the trip, but knowing Roy's and Dad's skill at fishing, we had brought tuna along, and had that for supper.

We had seen several groups of campers today. Two Forest Service friends rode by camp just after we got here, and one group of seven Wyoming girl scouts were hiking back to Dickenson Park. Both groups stopped to visit a bit, and we were grateful to find that Girl Scouts don't just sell cookies, but actually get out and compete for such activities as alpine backpacking. They mentioned that last week they had taken a cross-country bike tour.

We asked the Forest Service friends about Piney, and one thought he had seen her, and tried to get her to follow him, but she wouldn't. He planned to look for her the next day as he went back to Dickenson Park, and if he found her, he would take her back to Lander and have her kept for us. We then quit worrying about Piney, assuming she would be well taken care of.

About supper time, it began raining, so we hurried with our eating which we did under the tent. Since it was quite cool, we got into bed early to ensure keeping warm.

Friday, July 27, 1973

Today began with a hee-haw from Hannibal wanting his oats, and it was the most humorous sound, because spirit donkeys braying back in the form of echoes from the canyon walls in a unison chorus embellished the morning. It was a good day!
Starting a fire after the rain, especially when we had forgotten to put wood under our shelter, took some time. The breakfast menu included oatmeal, Tang and hot biscuits, the last of which promoted a great deal of patience from the hungering campers. However, after trying the first batch of 8 biscuits, Mom had another batch ready to go in the Dutch oven which was already hot, and since we didn't have to share the fire with other kettles, besides the fact we had already learned from the first experience, the chore was quickly accomplished to the delight of everyone. The biscuits were every bit as good as any baked in the most modern oven. Even Hannibal mooched a biscuit with honey on it, and begged for more.

We discussed medieval, European, colonial and Mexican culinary techniques so the children might appreciate heritages, and realize how comfortable our homes are, as well as learn how things can be done, even without the latest conveniences.
After breakfast, the men went fishing and the ladies set about camp chores. We did the dishes, put on a pot of beans, since we were staying here today and they would have time to cook, and then took baths and washed all the clothing we three girls had   on!

The guys returned with no fish, and although Mom hadn't

planned on chili beans for lunch (they were for dinner) we just had a later lunch and ate them, along with some potatoes and gray, onion and cornbread fried on the pancake griddle. Ymmm!

Immediately after we ate, rain came again. It had been threatening for some time, but it didn't pour until we had finished the dishes. Most of our wash was dry, or almost, so we gathered it in, and spread the damp pieces under the tent to finish drying.

The rain subsided for a while, and then came another moment of grandeur for the Dutch oven. Mom made a spice cake, and we heaped the lid of the Dutch oven with hot coals and took turns fanning them until hot buttered cake was ready to eat!
We brought out the maps and studied them, plotting tomorrow's course. Early in the morning we plan to pack up and hike to Macon Lake, about 2 ½ miles.

Dusk found us roasting marshmallows, and telling stories around the campfire. Dad was first to bed, and everyone else followed shortly.

Saturday, July 28, 1973

Hannibal awoke everyone in the valley again with his morning greeting at 6:30. As soon as a fire was started, everyone was up and about the chores of breaking down camp. Mom had breakfast of pancakes ready in short order, and we were loaded on the trail by 8:30.

Hannibal carried almost everything, except the bedrolls and clothing this time, and it made trail easier for us all. After a while, though, as we climbed, the packs seemed heavier and heavier, and we were wondering how we had carried so much before.

As we came down the side of a mountain on our way to Washakie Lake, we came to South Fork River which offered a multitude of interests. First, it was very beautiful, and coming out of ice and snow-fed lakes, very cold, teased with the offer of good fishing, AND had no bridge. Br-r-r-r. Dad suggested we take off our waffle-stompers and socks and wade across. Just before this, Roy walked to the edge of the river to survey the problem, with Hannibal right behind. It was 30 feet across, knee-deep and COLD!

The rest of us took off our foot gear, but it was tough walking on all those rocks with pants rolled up, and heavy packs on our backs. No one lost footing as we carefully picked our way, shivering all the while. Dad decided to throw his boots to shore and just as he started to throw, he slipped, and the boot went straight up in the air, and landed on the edge of the water. On the other side, we dried our fee and put on our dry shoes and socks—except Roy, who had wet fee the rest of the day. It was surprising how warm the grass felt after that icy wading.
We met a group of five or six hikers who seemed to have the same dilemma about crossing, and finally just waded across with shoes on.

Dad fly fished the stream a few minutes while Hannibal grazed from the lovely green meadow, and the rest of us relaxed before the next climb. The stream offered no encouragement for fishing, so we donned our packs and trekked on.

At Washakie Lake, Dad tried fishing again. He snuck up behind a small pine on the shore and offered a "Royal Coachman" fly to two lovely native goldens, but they didn't care for the menu and headed for deep water. He didn't give up immediately, but soon decided we could catch as many fish on the rocky trails, so we began again.

The ascent from Washakie Lake was somewhat similar to a painter climbing a ladder with a bucket of paint in one hand

and brush in the other while wearing ice skates! We did have a moment of bird-a-terrarianism-watching a little mountain wren try to distract us from her babies, who were nested under a rock.

With huffs and puffs, we finally topped the ridge that gave us a view of Macon Lake, Washakie Pass and a small no-name lake on the left. The splendor of this little alpine pocket is indeed awesome. We cast about some timberline pine shrubs for an appropriate place to make camp and then nestled our awning under the largest of the dwarfed trees, made camp, then Dad and Roy went fishing.

Success was finally realized! Dad caught about a 1 ½ pound golden and a small one about ¾ pound, which we fried immediately. The red meat of native trout freshly caught and fried was delicious! We also had a combination soup thickened with alfalfa sprouts and mushrooms, which in itself, was quite tasty.

No matter what time we eat—any meal except breakfast, it seems either to be threatening rain, or raining, hailing or sleeting! Today, it has managed to hail twice since we setup camp. Mosquitoes are terrible here—worse than anywhere we have been.

Our treat for tonight was Dad's favorite. Popcorn! He is always good at making it, but it never tasted better than tonight, and he didn't even burn the pan.

All the lakes we have seen are beautiful, but Macon Lake is in a category all its own in its uniqueness. The water is crystal clear, but in-depth, green and in moments of stillness, reflecting rocky cliffs, patches of snow, dwarfed pines and landmarks such as Washakie Peak, and Washakie Pass. The shore of this natural wonder is a jumble of promiscuously scattered granite boulders of every imaginable size and configuration, most of them with tout-haven pools between. Three major snow fields fed the lake.

Pink snow, to many people, belongs in Ripley's "Believe it or Not," but this snow is actually pink, and is made so by small organisms that thrive on these conditions provided by a very delicate balance of nature.

Bedtime snack was Tang, mixed with icy lake water. It tasted so like fresh orange juice!

No other campers are around Macon Lake. It seems to be less accessible than the others, and we're wondering how Hannibal will fare through the sea of boulders tomorrow.

Sunday, July 29, 1973

Our mountain canary alarm clock went off at an unreasonably early hour—between 5:00 and 6:00. Dad just wished him well, and went back to sleep. The second alarm went off about 7:00, so we crawled out and started a fire.

We had good intentions, but we were terribly slow getting everything done, perhaps due to dread of the sharp incline, boulder fields, and snow pack which lay ahead of us on Washakie Pass. Breakfast was oatmeal, hot biscuits and honey and Tang.

In spite of 50 thumbs, we finally managed to break camp and be on our way by shortly before 10:00. We had gone about ½ a mile straight up, when an ominous bank of dark clouds boiled over the pass. We took shelter on the lee side of a huge granite slab, covered ourselves with our awning, and sat out a minor deluge. When it ceased to rumble, and rain, we stuck our heads out and saw a patch of blue over the pass, which meant "sic-em tiger." So, 5 tigers and one donkey headed up!

Our trail, like a vanishing species, vanished! Dad went ahead and set the course so we didn't wind up backtracking out of a boulder patch or crevasse. Three eternities later we hit the last big snow field that we hoped would bring us to the summit. It was so steep that Roy led Hannibal in a traversing zigzag course. Hannibal was very careful with his footing, for had he slipped, we would have been picking pieces of donkey out of the boulder field far below.

We had a granola feast, and celebration atop Washakie Pass, and marveled at the splendor of creation. We got our breath and started our descent. Somewhere down the west side of Washakie Pass, the trail became so faint we lost it, but Dad knew roughly the lay of where Skull Lake should be, so he led us down game trails, pointing out elk, moose, deer and bear tracks along the way. We stopped for leisure in several little alpine meadows to relax and let Hannibal graze in the lush green grass, since he had seen very little of such the las few days.

We final arrived at Skull Lake, about 2:30, and setup our nicest camp so far—managing to eat between rain storms. All facilities were excellent, and Dad decided to see if conditions were also right for fishing. Yes, they were! He brought back 11 nice size pan friers, but since we had eaten, we saved them for breakfast.

We had our Sunday worship service. Roy led singing, and we read scriptures and had the Lord's Supper. Before this we had about an hour study in the Book of Acts, which we began studying at the beginning of the trip.

Another storm began to threaten about 9:00, so we scurried to our sleeping bags under the shelter to stay warm. The wind was rather vigorous, and our tent did a lot of flapping, but stayed secure, and a good night's sleep was had by all.

Monday, July 30, 1973

Today was planned as a day in camp for fishing, bathing, washing and hair shampooing. We didn't set our alarm—Hannibal, so slept in until 7:00.

Dad is really hooked on biscuits, so we had them again for breakfast, along with fish and malt-o-meal. After breakfast, Dad took Roy down to the lake to teach him the rudiments of fly fishing. Roy caught on quickly enough and shortly Dad left him to fish solo. During the morning, Roy caught 12 more fish, after Dad caught the first to show him how.

Dad decided we needed to stock pile more firewood, especially since there was fire wood here when we came. We saddled Hannibal and found four big, dry tree limbs, tied nylon rope around them, and Hannibal pulled them into camp. Even though we didn't cover any miles, Hannibal earned his sugar cubes again, and there will be plenty of firewood for us and the next hikers, fulfilling the code of the mountain.

We don't know whether it was out of boredom, or ambition, but Dad periodically sawed and chopped firewood all day.
We visited with some of a mountaineering group of 28 from Chicago who are coming into this area for a two-week climbing expedition. The club has been climbing mountains all over the Rockies since 1928.

Today was a record! Not one drop of rain, and we have had two meals besides breakfast without it raining one drop, or even clouding up! The wash got dry, and everyone had baths and shampooed hair.

The men repaired and lubricated the fly reel, and went back to the lake for another fly fishing lesson for Roy. They caught six, but turned them loose since we had all we could eat for supper. The fish went well with the beans Mom carefully cooked all

215

day.

A casual evening around the campfire followed roasting marshmallows and just visiting before retiring to bed. A blowing storm hit just as we tucked ourselves nighty-night.

Tuesday, July 31, 1973

We were lazy and slow getting up, and then had trouble getting a fire started, due to the dampness, even though we had put the wood under the tent to keep dry. Everything seemed to be soggy here from all the recent moisture.

Finally broke down camp and loaded up about 9:45. Hannibal walked without coaxing, and we made very good time. At a stream, some waded across, but Mom took off her shoes and had to be helped across because the green scum on the rocks was so slippery she was afraid she would fall, pack and all, in the icy water.

We arrived at Marm's Lake in one and a half hours, a two and a half mile, pleasant walk from Skull Lake, and Dad and Mom pretended to be dudes while the children picked a camp site and setup camp with the idea of keeping their "dudes" happy and comfortable.

Lunch was served shortly, since everything is much dryer here, and a fire was quickly started. For the first time since we began our trip, the fire was uncomfortably warm, and allowed to go out between meals. It was so warm that the children decided to go swimming, but each time they would go down to the water, the sun would go behind a cloud and the wind would come up, causing the idea of swimming to be less appealing. They would scramble back under the tent for a few moments, and try again later. All that was ever accomplished was a little wading.

They then resorted to whittling. Roy tried to amputate his

thumb, and the first aid kit came in handy for the first time on the trip. Dad was the doctor, and the patient survived. The accident didn't seem to dampen the girls' ambition for whittling, and they each created various totem-like animals.

As boredom approached epidemic proportions, and having the first aid booklet handy after Roy's accident, a first aid class seemed to be in order. We read and discussed the entire book!

We brought music staff paper along, and the children used it to learn music theory. They begged for practice in ear training too, something Mom never dreamed would come to pass. She would sing intervals, and scales to them and they would take turns identifying them.

Dad caught a ten inch rainbow trout shortly after lunch, but was never able to catch any companions for him. No one seems too eager to eat fish today, anyway! Laziness is the order of the day!

This has been the nicest day we've had, weather-wise. No wind or rain, and the fire has been the best ever, with smoke rising up instead of in everyone's face. The wood is dry and burns beautifully, a real phenomenon to us, since moisture has been so plentiful during the whole trip. The coals were perfect for roasting marshmallows, an activity the children never tire of. Roy caught a companion fish for the one Dad caught— breakfast food.

Mosquitoes are hungrier than some places we've been, but Macon Lake was champion in that category. We are retiring under clear skies with no storm threatening—another first!

Wednesday, August 1, 1973

We had a casual breakfast of fish, biscuits and oatmeal. We were all anxious to hit the trail, although we planned to go only to Dad's Lake, which was one-half mile from Marm's Lake where we had camped. However, since we were at the north end of Marm's Lake, and hiked to the south end of Dad's Lake, it was considerably farther than one-half mile.

Dad's Lake is very irregularly shaped with the shoreline a combination of rocky cliffs and swampy marshes. It has several islands with lovely trees, beckoning to visitors to swim out to them. The outlet of the lake is most spectacular. The water course divides itself several times and the many deep pools at the bottom of cascading waterfalls hold a variety in size, of trout lurking to deceive the wary fisherman.

While Dad and Roy were fishing the outlet, a rain and hail storm hit. But, they sat it out high and dry under a clump of pines, which served as an umbrella. Meanwhile, back at camp, the womenfolk took shelter under the tent while the heaviest hail and rain storm during our outing poured down. Ronda got out and trenched around the tent to keep us from being drowned out.

The guys brought in four nice Browns, two rather small, but two were about a foot in length, and they were plenty for supper. Just as we were ready to eat, as is customary (except rarely), another storm matured and we ate under the tent, while the dishpan full of water covered the fire and at the same time heated for washing the dishes when the storm subsided.

Mom washed dishes between storms and since Dad had promised popcorn to us, he kept true to his promise, although he had to pop the corn in torrents of rain and hail. Everyone enjoyed the popcorn this time, especially since it was a nice bedtime snack, and Dad had to really time things well in order to get the job done. We crawled into sleeping bags to keep warm, and it was almost as dark anyway.

Not long after we were in bed, the fourth storm of the evening hit, and although Ronda had trenched around the tent, water had been seeping in, and we suddenly realized the mattress pads were wet, and gradually getting the sleeping bags wet. We knew we had some sheet plastic with us, so Dad in his underwear, and bare feet, got out of his sleeping bag and standing out in the hail and rain, shivering to his toes, began searching through the paniers.

Not readily finding the plastic, he grabbed a new box of foil as a substitute, and we lay it out over the mattresses to keep the moisture from soaking through the sleeping bags.

Thursday, August 2, 1973

We weren't in too much of a hurry to get started today, for we didn't hav far to go to Meeks Lake, and we dreaded trying to start a fire after all the moisture from yesterday. We had saved back some good wood, and protected it under the tent, so it wasn't as difficult as we expected.

A few drovers and a band of about 300 sheep with sheep dogs kept things interesting for a while as they drove their sheep up the trail into the high country.

We had a pleasant hike of about four miles across lovely meadows and forests to Meeks Lake. The terrain changed noticeably as we descended the high mountain area. Trees are larger and more plentiful, boulders are more sparse, and fire burns much easier.

Each day we have encountered other hiker and back packers; the only time no one has been near our camp was at Macon Lake. As we arrived there in the afternoon, we got a glimpse of hikers going over the top of Washakie Pass, and as we left the next morning, we spotted people approaching the Lake, but it was our most obscure camp of the trip.

About 4:00 we decided to hike down to Big Sandy Guard Camp and see what was there, about two and a half miles away. We enjoyed the walk without packs and the trail became more and more marked as we got closer to civilization. Not far from the trail head, Gene Hunt was gathering wood to take back to his family's camp, so we helped carry it. They had come up to spend the night and fish as they waited for us to arrive, and be ready to go back to Lander tomorrow. We had no more than arrived when a rain storm hit, and we went in their tent to wait out the storm. We made plans to meet at our camp for lunch tomorrow, after the guys fished a while, and during a lull in the storm at a little before 6:00, we hurried back to Meeks Lake.

It was difficult to start a fire after the downpour, but we managed to get the job done, and have supper. Roasting marshmallows was especially fun because Hannibal was edging closer and closer to camp and Ronda decided to give him a taste. It was a comical sight watching him try to get the sticky stuff off his lips, but he loved it and begged for more.

Friday, August 3, 1973

We arose, eager to return to civilization, yet nostalgically remembering the beauty of our journey. Everyone set about the routine of rolling up the pads and sleeping bags, and preparing for guests for lunch. Around 11:00 a.m., Gene Hunt and his family arrived. Gene tried his hand at fishing, the children admired and petted Hannibal, and Mom and Barbara visited as they prepared the last of the food rations for lunch. We couldn't resist giving them a sample of biscuits from the Dutch oven.

Our eagerness to get home must have showed, because everyone was helping pack dishes and cooking utensils away as fast as they were dried. Hannibal had a lighter load now, with most of the food gone, so little Jackie Hunt rode him back to the trail head as the rest of us walked, except for Christi, who rode on her dad's backpack.

At Big Sandy, there were people all over the place! Friday afternoon meant people were arriving for the weekend. When people asked us how long we had been out, we realized we must look rather weather-beaten with our sunburned faces and dirty clothes.

It was a good thing we had a big truck to load everything, because we needed it with two family's provisions, a donkey and all of us. We tried a dirt bank to load Hannibal, but it wasn't the proper slant and we couldn't get close enough to it. Then, Dad backed up to a rock and Hannibal climbed it with the grace of a stunt man, and the poise of a ballerina, and got into the truck, fully realizing he was going home! We all shared a lump in our throats, and mutual awe as we crawled into the truck and began the journey home. We had to have one last rainfall—on the way home.

Now, when we look up into the mountains from our picture window, we have a deep sense of appreciation for the creation with which we have communed.

While this is the end of the book, I hope you will stay in touch! You can do that by connecting with me on Facebook at https://www.facebook.com/hazel.ramsbotham

If you enjoyed *88 Keys to Living a Long and Purposeful Life*, please take the time to tell others about your reading experience by providing an Amazon review. Very few people take the time to write reviews and they are so important to book buying decisions. Future readers, and I, would greatly appreciate it.

Be sure to visit **ProduceMyBook.com** to learn how I FINALLY got the book inside me written and produced!

ProduceMyBook.com: Concept to customer non-fiction books in as little as 8 weeks without the author ever typing a word of the manuscript!

Made in the USA
Coppell, TX
10 March 2022

74801996R00128